When DRAG RACING *met* COUNTRY MUSIC

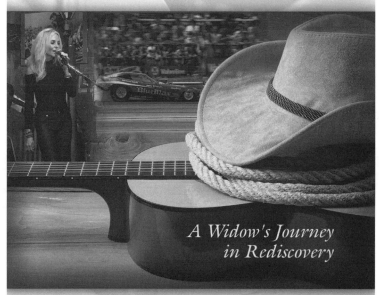

A Widow's Journey in Rediscovery

TERRI LYNN SCHMIDT

TERRI LYNN SCHMIDT

When DRAG RACING *met* COUNTRY MUSIC

A Widow's Journey in Rediscovery

TERRI LYNN SCHMIDT

TERRI LYNN SCHMIDT

To my beautiful daughters,
Hillary and Hailey,
who walked through this journey with me.
You are stronger than you can possibly imagine
and more precious to me
than you will ever know.

To Schmidt'em,
my Knight in Shining Armor,
thank you.
You showed me a life I only dreamed I could live.
You demonstrated the Fruits of the Spirit
to your family and friends
with honesty and integrity.

When DRAG RACING *met* COUNTRY MUSIC

CONTENTS

TERRI LYNN SCHMIDT

CONTENTS *(continued)*

ACKNOWLEDGEMENTS

Where would I be without my heavenly Father?
He has wooed me, He has saved me,
He has provided for me,
and He has protected me.
He is my closest best Friend
and He is my husband.
He knows me better than anyone ...
and still He loves me.

PREFACE

Do knights in shining armor still exist? You bet they do. A knight swept me off my feet with a smile at a water fountain.

Our worlds could not have been more different. Harry was a Highland Park Scot graduate and I, a Grand Prairie Gopher graduate. In 1965, Harry's senior high year, I was born. There was a twenty-year difference in our ages. Our very first date was dinner at Gleneagles Country Club. I sat across the table from this handsome gentleman wearing golf slacks, a Rolex, wearing a grin and thought, "*I have absolutely nothing in common with this guy and besides that, he is too old for me, but he is just so handsome. Especially when he smiles!*"

Harry was much too sophisticated and intelligent, and there I sat wearing a fuzzy sweater covered in large colored stones to match my huge '80s hair! All I wanted to do was be on stage and sing. There was no way I could possibly find anything in common with him. He was soft spoken, yet he had a wisdom and gentleness about him that drew me in. Though I had seen the picture of a race car over his desk when I went to his office to thank him for flowers he had sent to me, it would be many years later before I fully understood the legend of the Blue Max funny car Harry had owned. We parted for three years when I returned to Nashville. Little did I know he was watching over me from a distance ... the entire time.

God had a plan.

The collection of writings in the pages that follow were written a few months before Harry's passing on April 30, 2012, to present. The editor of the newspaper that prints my column soon recognized a pattern. Throughout the six years of writing about all matters of the heart in my column, Beauty Is Fleeting: *Inside Matters*, I had touched on different stages of the grieving process, reflecting upon my personal journey. It had not been my intention, but after going back and revisiting a few in print from 2012, the year Harry died, I realized that she was right.

When DRAG RACING *met* COUNTRY MUSIC

Some were sad, some joyful and humorous, and some were simply matter-of-fact. All of them ending with Scripture directing our focus toward God's Word.

Friends and family began to ask where they could read all of my collective writings, so I decided to bring them together here. Some reflect the beauty of God's creation He shares with us along the journey. Others highlight personal growth in rediscovering our identity as His children ... learning how to hold on to hope after the loss of a loved one.

My prayer is that if you are a widow or widower, or you have lost a loved one, this book will speak to your heart in the midst of your personal journey. I believe we all grieve in our own individual way and in our own timing. There is no right or wrong way. As believers though, we do not grieve as the world grieves for we grieve with a hope. Our faith and hope lie in the promises from God that we will be reunited with our loved ones when we are all called up in heaven together.

First Thessalonians 4:13 says, "Brothers and sisters, we do not want you to be uninformed about those who sleep in death, so that you do not grieve like the rest of mankind, who have no hope" (NIV). These brothers and sisters are those who have placed their saving faith in Jesus Christ—the true, living Son of our holy God. The "rest of mankind" referenced in the Scripture are the nonbelievers. They mourn with the mind-set that they will never see their loved ones again. That would be just so awful to have no hope. Our Father has you in the palm of His hand and hides you under His mighty wings. Lean into Him. He sees your pain and knows it very well. You were created in His image.

Before sharing with you the moment when I became a widow, a single mom, and an empty nester all in the same day, pictures need to be drawn and painted—canvases of Harry's life before mine and mine before his, how our two completely different worlds found their way to each other that exact moment in time at a water fountain.

Let's begin painting.

TERRI LYNN SCHMIDT

INTRODUCTION

Noticing someone standing behind me, hearing the swishing sound of a golf club, then turning around, I found myself gazing into the eyes of a tall, dark, and handsome man sporting a huge grin. I was pouring old coffee creamer down the drain, and Harry was standing there smiling, swinging his club waiting for me to finish so he could get a drink. There we were. Standing at the water fountain. I revisited that fountain the week after Harry died.

It's still there.

I hid the fountain with my body so he could not see me poking the awful milk through the drain holes. The sun had bronzed his face and arms after a round of golf. I think back now and realize that his smile was probably because he knew exactly what I was doing! Who was this handsome man? "The most eligible bachelor in the building," I was told by my coworkers.

A few days later, a dozen red roses would appear on my desk at work. The notecard in the flower box simply said HMS. A few weeks later, a guitar showed up in the reception area after he learned I was an entertainer. It was 1986. Five years later I would become Mrs. Harry Schmidt.

A LEGEND
in the Making

*H*arry Maxson Schmidt was born on December 25, 1944, Christmas Day, in Atlanta, Georgia. There were no rooms available at the hospital when his mother went into labor. Betsy gave birth to her middle child in the hospital hallway behind make-do privacy screens. His big brother Don was in Dallas, Texas with his grandparents at the time. Harry's father was working with the Plantation Pipeline Company. Susan, his little sister, was born a few years later in Dallas.

Harry spent his elementary, junior high, and high school years growing up in the town of Highland Park. His mother had attended Hockaday, was a member of the Junior League of Dallas, and a graduate of Stephens College. She was a committed Dallas philanthropist. Charles Schmidt, Harry's father, was a mechanical engineer with a BS degree in petroleum and gas from Oklahoma University and a Master's degree from the University of Texas. The Schmidt family owned a steel metal company called Delta Metals, Inc. Charles flew quite often with his partners on business matters in their company plane. Betsy became one of Dallas' first female pilots when she took lessons so she could surprise her husband and fly their plane while the men worked. Harry's family were members of the Episcopalian church.

I remember Harry sharing with me his love of hunting and fishing with his father at Coon Creek in Athens, where they had a membership and a few of their family members had homes. (I still have the picture from one of those fishing moments—Harry holding his fish so proudly). Some of his most treasured memories were playing ball in the neighboring empty lot by his home with his longtime neighbor and friend, Bart. He and Bart remained lifetime friends. Summer camps with the YMCA kept Harry busy as a young man. I have the notes he sent to his parents signed, "Yours Truly, Harry Schmidt" (as if they had no idea who was writing to them).

Another memory Harry shared was how as a young boy, he would play in the large fountain in the front yard of the DeGoyler home, which is now part of the Dallas Arboretum. He would call it a swimming pool. His Uncle Jack Maxson married a daughter in the DeGoyler family, so their families would all gather together for the holidays. When Harry was a young man, his father taught him and his siblings how to build go-carts. Inheriting his father's mechanical mindset, innovation, and love for speed would ultimately launch him into a career of racing.

A family with a lot of fascinating history helped shape Harry into the man he became. Growing up, he spent a lot of time with his family and grandparents. Harry's paternal grandfather, Elmer Schmidt, was vice president of Lone Star Gas Company in the 1950s, and his maternal grandfather, Harry I. Maxson, was instrumental in organizing Universal Life Insurance Company and aided in the chapel and rectory build at St. Mark's School of Dallas. Mr. Maxson played an intricate part of the startup group for The University Club atop of the Sante Fe Building. Harry's maternal great-grandfather, Willis Maxson, was vice president of the southern division of the Sante Fe Railroad and his other maternal great-grandfather, Charles Noel Flagg, was an accomplished Paris-trained portrait painter. One of his most noted pieces of work was the painting of his next door neighbor, Samuel Clemens (aka Mark Twain). His portait of Mark Twain hangs at the Metropolitian Muesum of Art in New York City and was featured on the cover of Life Magazine in 1968. Other paintings of his can be found at the Vanderbilt's Biltmore Home in North Carolina. The Schmidt and Maxson women were just as strong in their own rights. Heavily involved in society, educated, and involved in the philanthropic communities. Harry's aunts and his mother also painted and sculpted.

At the age of sixteen, Harry and his family's lives were devastated when Charles was killed in his private plane in route to a business meeting in Arkansas. Unable to express inward emotions, Harry acted out with his actions. His mother found a program that involved manual labor on a naval ship to help get him back on course. Harry actually thought he was going on a private cruise until he arrived and discovered there were other delinquents on the ship as well. Upon completing the program, he returned home to finish high school and went on to Westminster College in Missouri. Harry's mother would remarry twelve years later to a retired three-star major general of the Marine Corps, Edwin B. Wheeler. Ed had four daughters, so Harry inherited four more sisters.

Susan, Betsy, and Harry

Harry's love for fast cars surfaced in his late teens and early twenties and quickly became his focus—something his mother was not too keen on him doing. She had made sure he was educated in all the ways of becoming a gentleman, polished in manners, and knew how to dance with the young ladies at cotillion. Many years would go by before Betsy would acknowledge Harry's passion for drag racing. Their relationship was estranged for a season as a result. Harry married a high school sweetheart, and together they had two beautiful children, Harry Jr. and Heather. After his marriage was severed, he poured all of his attention into racing, launching his first round of cars in the late 1960s with Jake Johnston behind the wheel. During this time the car was decorated with only his name and sponsors.

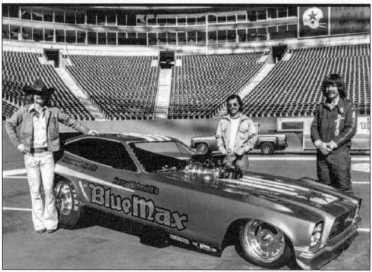

Harry Schmidt and Raymond Beadle

When DRAG RACING *met* COUNTRY MUSIC

After watching the World War I movie about a pilot setting his sights on Germany's highest medal of valor, The Blue Max, something occurred to Harry. His last name was German, his race car was blue, and his middle name was Maxson. Right then he revamped his car so it sported a new paint scheme and title of the 'Blue Max' in the funny car category with Richard Tharp as his driver. The Blue Max quickly

rose to fame with National Hot Rod (NHRA), and International Hot Rod (IHRA), title wins. As owner and chief mechanic— and with new driver Raymond Beadle behind the wheel— Harry and his Blue Max team took the title win over Don "Snake" Prudhom- me in 1975. The winnings and championship titles landed Beadle and Schmidt a spot in the NHRA and IHRA Halls of Fame. With his success came a respect from his mother that he so desperately desired. Gradually, Harry grew tired of the race circuit lifestyle (traveling hundreds of days a year from track to track) and wanted to retire after the famed championship title.

In 1978, Harry retired as a drag racing pioneer and one of the Legends of the Quarter Mile. Still in his early forties, he tried his hand in a new business adventure in a completely different field. After working for a friend and realizing he had a natural inclination for selling, in 1983 he launched his own wholesale company, HMS Fine Jewelry. Rapidly, his company became a success with thousands of clients all over the country. Three years into starting his new company, after a day of playing golf at Prestonwood CC (of course, he had been their club champion) and before taking the elevator up to his second-floor office, he stopped to take a drink at a water fountain. That's when he saw me.

TERRI LYNN SCHMIDT

MUSIC
Was My Life

*B*orn on the first day of spring, March 20, 1965, in Grand Prairie, Texas, I was the middle child. We all *know* how special middle children are. As the saying goes, "Rules were created because of that middle child!" The firstborn had no rules, and the last born threw the rules out the window. I love my two sisters. We are three very different personalities. Upbringing and family dynamics played a big part of memories that are embedded in my mind. My very fondest memories were trips to Abilene to visit the Vaughn family. Water skiing, camping, and frog gigging! Also, we frequently visited two of the most favorite people in my life, my maternal grandparents, MaMaw and PaPaw. C.D. and Edna Wingrove. There was always a hug and a home-cooked meal complete with sweet tea and green onions waiting for us when we arrived. Our family would play games of dominos, rings, cards, or spoons for hours. PaPaw was a hard worker and MaMaw raised four daughters.

Funny thing about memories is that after hearing stories told over and over throughout the years, the incident that happened to one person somehow became something that happened to the other. The toothpaste that was slung and landed on one sister's eyelashes as she walked through the door actually landed on another's. Weeks and weeks spent in the hospital with pneumonia happened really to just one sister, but somehow that's not the one who was actually ill, as the story goes. *Was that Tammy or Tina who stood nose to the corner for hours ... or was that actually me? I am so confused!* I am positive we will argue the facts and details forever!

My older sister was two years old and I was one when our parents went through a divorce. Our dad, Don Cox, was a bass guitar musician, always traveling, performing. His brother was an acoustic guitar player and had occasionally opened for Willy Nelson. My paternal grandmother O'Neda and her sister hosted a radio show on which they also performed. Though I did not know my dad until my later years, I knew that I had acquired my love for music and singing by inheriting the gene he passed down to me. I can still look in the mirror and see my dad's hazel eyes. My paternal great-grandmother was one-fourth Cherokee. I also have her eyes. My Mother told me that I started singing at the age of two. Pulling my thumb out of my mouth just in time for the chorus I would announce, along with the radio, "Don't Touch Me Unless You Love Me." Standing in front of the television with my small hands on the screen, I danced and sang along to "She's A Lady." Tom Jones probably taught me how to dance, and my rhythm most likely came from the Cherokee blood running through my veins.

Several years later after my parents' divorce, my mother Sherry remarried E.C. and soon my little sister Tina was born. Boy how we fought over who was going to get to hold her in their lap for pictures. We just adored her cuteness. Through the years my stepdad began building our relationship with him by taking us fishing, one daughter at a time. Always we would wake early, rush to get dressed, hop in the pickup truck and make a pit stop for worms. Our special treat was a liter of Big Red soda all to ourselves. As Daddy began to work longer hours, our times spent with him began to decrease. Life seemed normal though. One exception would be an incident when our family German Shepherd was shot and killed in our backyard. No longer feeling safe in our neighborhood, we made a move pretty quickly after that.

There were incidents and a lot of moving during my most impressionable years: another divorce in our family due to an affair and alcoholism, several moves following, and food stamps until my mother, Sherry, could acquire a job. We took taxis to school a few times when we didn't have transportation. I remember standing in line at the grocery store, looking around hoping none of our friends would walk up and see us tearing off the stamps to pay for our groceries. My stepdad had left our family in a bind with no funds.

As a stay-at-home mom Mother had sewn and made a lot of our school costumes and homecoming outfits. She was a very active member of the PTA and was a highly talented, respected, beautiful woman amongst her friends and family. Her award-winning pies always won contests because of her sky-high meringue. (With the exception of the one year Tina Lee snuck into the refrigerater in the middle of the night and ate all the meringue!) With the divorce and Mother beginning to work, the dynamics of our everyday life as we had known it, had changed. She supported all of our extracurricular activities, housing, and food by herself. She is one of the strongest women I know.

Through elementary, junior high, and high school, I sang in choir classes at every level available to me: musicals, both in school and community theatre, talent shows, local singing competitions, and pageants. I sang in a few saloons in high school. Rocking with a garage band at a pool party was short-lived, but exciting. Assuming I would excel at every competition I entered, because of the music inclination passed down to me (you know, the "natural talent" syndrome), I did not put forth the amount of work and effort it took to be the best I could be. Deep down inside I knew it. I still pressed forward, but after my parents' divorce, I went into a silent personal survival mode. My grades began to fall. Although our family had attended church while I was very young, it wasn't until high school at the age of sixteen at a church revival I was invited to, that I asked Jesus to by my Lord and Savior. I was heading down a path of uncertainty and God gave me a hope and promise for my future. I was baptized in an Assembly of God church with friends as my witness. I made an effort to stay connected in church, but it was difficult as I did not have a church home and had to rely upon friends to invite and take me. I became what the kids at school would label me, a radical Christian or "Jesus freak". That was okay, they were right.

Two more years of high school and a semester of junior college later, an audition tour with Opryland USA from Nashville came through Dallas. Nashville became my new focus when a spot in a show production was offered to me. At nineteen, my life was about to change forever. Still, with my low self-esteem, I had convinced myself that I had barely made the cut. A majority of the others who had auditioned had been formally trained. Though I had taken vocal lessons, I still was astounded that I was chosen. I remember going down on my knees on February 7, 1984, in tears, thanking God for giving me the Nashville opportunity. Although it hurt to leave my family and close friends behind, it was the best thing that could have ever happened to me. God still had a plan for my life, and singing was to be part of it.

TERRI LYNN SCHMIDT

As I crossed the Tennessee line, I had no idea all the people I would meet, the places I would go, and the opportunities I would have. Performers from all over the United States were joined together to be the cast of *Country Music USA*. Different personalities and different levels of talent made up our show collaboration. Together we performed for the Gaylords at the Oklahoma State Fair, Delta Airlines, State Farm, Toyota, Ford, and on the General Jackson Showboat for an All Sports Hall of Fame event. Several of our shows were reserved and performed on the Grand Ole Opry stage through the Opryland Talent Agency.

DOD Show in Honduras

The highlighted memories of my career were receiving stage presence training by Minnie Pearl on the Opry stage, having Loretta Lynn come onto our rehearsal to show us how Hank Williams would have stood holding his guitar, and traveling to Central America through the Department of Defense to perform for our troops stationed in Cuba, Panama, and Honduras. Another memorable performance was our singing alongside Brenda Lee and Lee Greenwood to "God Bless the USA." We had a friend who played fiddle for Roy Acuff, and it was an honor sitting in Roy's dressing room and watching what took place in between shows. At that time, the Nashville Network was on air and many of us had a guest performance on the Porter Waggoner at Opryland Show.

When DRAG RACING *met* COUNTRY MUSIC

Notable music producers would come out to scout our show throughout the years. When I was overlooked for a conversation of a record label opportunity, still in denial of my God gifted talent, I once again silently withdrew. Our country show just oozed with talent. One of those talented singers was Steve, who would go on to saddle up his horse into the "Great Adventure" of receiving Dove after Dove awards. Chonda used her pure humor and testimony to produce DVDs as a Christian comedian. Marty would sing lead for Diamond Rio, the Little Texas boys would pen "God Blessed Texas," and Skip would write hit after hit for major recording artists. Chris married and joined the Out of the Grey group and would start "Walking by Faith and Not by Sight." Try comparing yourself to that lineup of talent. Mistake number one for sure. With my self-imposed disenchantment of the music industry and lack of confidence in my abilities, it became apparent to me that I needed to reevaluate my expectations. So, I went home.

Back in Dallas, I was only 21 and I knew I did not want to completely give up on my music career, but I needed to work while I regrouped. I took a part-time job as a loan processer for a mortgage company. The office was on the first floor of the building. There was a front entrance and a rear. One afternoon I stepped out that backdoor into the hallway and walked up to a water fountain. That's when I saw him.

TERRI LYNN SCHMIDT

TWO HEARTS
Commit

od had perfectly timed our divine appointment. He knew all the events surrounding both of our lives leading up to that very moment, and we were completely unaware. Though neither of us was walking closely with the Lord at the time, He never took His hands off that little girl who memorized Scripture when she was young. Or that little boy who carried the cross down the aisle as an altar boy. He began knitting our lives together, but it would be five years later before taking us down the path toward marriage. I had a lot of decisions to make at 21 years old and still held tight to my performing dream. Harry was patient.

In 1987, I returned to Nashville with a new mindset and excitement for two more years of performing at Opryland, traveling with a Christmas show tour and a month tour in Central America performing for the DOD. Harry continued to grow his company with great success. We kept our communication line open with hours of conversations by pay phone. Even high in the mountains of Honduras, before cell phones, he was able to reach me in the communications tent for conversation. There was still that wisdom, gentleness, and patience about Harry that I fell in love with. Faced with the decision between a music career or marriage, I made the decision to move back to Dallas permanently in 1989, and on April 20, 1991, I married my handsome knight.

On our wedding day, I wore Betsy's wedding gown. It was fifty years old and it fit me like a glove. What an honor to have worn the beautiful dress that Harry's mom had worn when she married Charles. She had led a life surrounded by beautiful dresses and beautiful people. Harry and I were married in her Dallas home. Eight months later, I was pregnant with our first child, and in August 1992, our daughter Hillary was born. We gave her the family name, Flagg, as her middle name. Another thirteen months later, we had our second daughter, Hailey Wingrove, named from the grandparents on my side of the family.

Harry and I raised our daughters in Dallas with the help of the Christian Learning Center at Prestonwood Baptist Church. God began to draw us closer and closer to Him and began showing us how to raise our family up in a Christian home. At the age of five, Hillary started attending Prestonwood Christian Academy on its opening day. On October 31, 1998, we joined the church as a family and were baptized there as well—the girls when they were younger and Harry and I together in 2004, after Harry gave his life to Christ. Our family was growing in the knowledge and faith in the Lord, both through discipleship and Bible study. With my passion for singing, I joined the Prestonwood choir when the campus was built in Plano. Harry continued his work with his jewelry company in the building he designed in Addison, and I became a "professional" volunteer at our girls' school as well as a stay-at-home mom taking care of our family. God's plan was beginning to unfold.

Throughout the years, before Harry officially sold HMS Jewelry and retired, we would take the girls out of school and travel with them across the country in our motor coach, homeschooling them through an online academy. This was our way of giving them access to hands-on learning and seeing the United States along the way. Off we would go for months at a time with two children, two dogs, in a bus with two bunkbeds and four slide-outs towing a Jeep. Trust me, we needed all that space! Harry and I created adventure for our family with river rafting, mountain hiking, jeep trailing, helicopter flights, biking, and visiting every National Park along our path. We became seasonal residents in Breckenridge, Colorado and attended Rocky Mountain Bible. In 2006 we went on our first mission trip as a family to the Amazon River in Brazil—a life-changing experience for all of us. God had a reason and a purpose for our years of traveling together building family memories with bonding time. Although Harry had to drag us out of town kicking and screaming at times, God knew what was around the bend. What was coming would be a devastating blow to our family. 17 years into our marriage, Harry was diagnosed with prostate cancer.

Hillary, Harry, Terri, and Hailey

TERRI LYNN SCHMIDT

After the initial shock of the news, we thought, *"Okay, we will figure this out and do what all is necessary to treat the cancer in its early stages"*. At this time our girls were in high school. We continued traveling together when Harry felt like it, but after a season of radiation treatments, the cancer returned. Harry made me cut off his hair. With a rapidly growing cancer cell, we realized we were going to have to take a more aggressive approach: surgery, chemo, more radiation, hormone therapy, cancer wellness center, clean organic healthy eating, stem cells, Procrit injections to increase red blood cells, and induced comas to relieve pain. There were emergency room visits in Dallas, Colorado, and Alabama. This became his and our family's new reality. A physician in Germany created a serum that Harry injected into himself along with taking drops on his tongue.

In Hillary's freshman year at the University of Alabama and Hailey's senior year of high school, ten days after our twenty-first wedding anniversary, on April 30, 2012, Harry was gone. His sweet body could no longer hold up or keep up with the pace of the spreading cancer cells. I could feel the presence of the Spirit. A stillness. Reverence. I sang Amazing Grace in his ear and quoted as many scriptures as I could recall in the moments before his heart stopped beating. I whispered, "You are a good man. You are a good father. You are a good husband. It is okay to go. You have surrounded the girls and me with strong men among your friends. You were right. I was wrong. You told me I would miss you when you were gone. You were so right. Please forgive me. I will always love you. Always." At 6:41 a.m., Harry took his last breath.

Tears. Silence. Tears. Pain.

Tears. Regret. Tears. Numb.

Repeat.

If you have ever heard a child screaming and wailing in pain, it is not a sound easily forgotten. Our children were limp and exhausted in the deepest pain they could possibly experience. I remember there were a lot of people in our house that morning. I'm still foggy on who was present. Pastors from Prestonwood and the Headmaster of PCA had come over a few days before to pray for and over Harry before his passing, and the days to come would demand preparation, time lines, and more pain. I had become a widow, a single mom, and an empty nester in that moment. Our children had become fatherless in that moment. A flood of memories came gushing through. Oh, how I longed for another chance of our water fountain meeting. I thanked God for the 21-year gift of marriage to my Knight wearing his new shiny armor, in Heaven.

Continually, I quoted 1 Corinthians 15:55 out loud: "O death, where is your victory? O death, where is your sting?" (NLT). And I reminded myself and my daughters that because Harry was a Christian, though dead, now he was more alive than ever. Cancer, as long as Harry was alive, was a constant reminder of death that had an attempted hold on him. Satan's intent was to kill and destroy. As a believing Christian, Harry knew his passing from life in his diseased body into the heavenly realm, the Enemy had lost—defeated by Harry's living in the presence of his Savior ... ALIVE. His Savior, Jesus Christ, had defeated death on the cross. Therefore the Enemy was defeated and deemed powerless. It still hurts. Yet my faith and hope in God's promise remain steadfast for those who mourn in Him. Amen.

One late afternoon after a long stay at the hospital, leaving Harry's side upon learning of his short time to live, I went home and hopped in the shower. I was finally able to let myself cry just as loud and hard as I needed to, repeating, "Father, Father, Father" over and over. Through my screaming and tears, I kept hearing my phone's ringtone, "Good Life," and began rushing to finish, so I could answer what I thought was an emergency hospital call. Hearing the ringtone stopping and starting again, I was certain it was an emergency. Quickly drying off and hopping out of the shower, I began looking for my phone. I couldn't find it anywhere. Finally, I found it. In the kitchen. Nowhere near hearing distance.

God was speaking to me. He affirmed that He was with my daughters and me in the midst of heartbreak and devastation. Harry was to belong to Him now, in Heaven. Immediately, I grabbed a piece of paper and began writing. My May column deadline was before Harry's funeral. The title? "A Good Life". Now, six years later still walking through this journey a grateful woman, my prayer is that you remain steadfast in your nearness to the Lord in your grieving. It is not an easy journey, Brother and Sister. God is the *only* hope and future we have. He reminds us that we are never alone. Know and recognize this truth:

God loves you and desires for you to keep your eyes fixed upon Him. His Son has walked your path. As God in the flesh, Jesus knows your pain. He is the High Priest that can sympathize with you. Trust Him. Lean on Him. Press into Him. Let Him cover you in the shadow of His mighty wings.

You. Are. Not. Alone.

> *"The LORD bless you and keep you; the LORD make*
> *His face shine upon you, and be gracious to you; the*
> *LORD lift up His countenance upon you, and give*
> *you peace."*

NUMBERS 6:24–26

And so ... the journey begins.

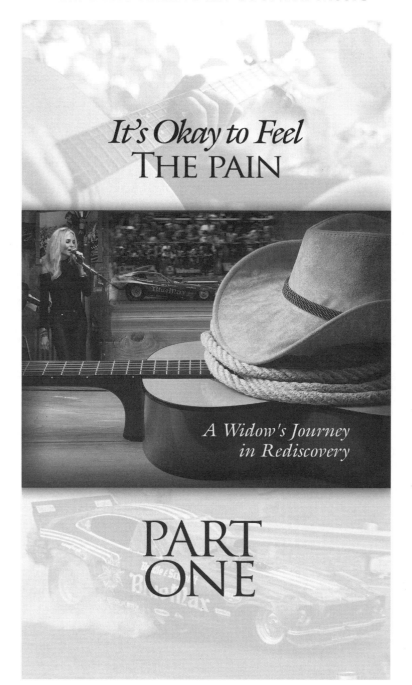

It's Okay to Feel
THE PAIN

*A Widow's Journey
in Rediscovery*

PART
ONE

TERRI LYNN SCHMIDT

Tears

*R*aindrops on a window running together and picking up speed join with other drops and quickly streak their way across the glass, then disappear off in the blurriness of my vision. Soon new drops take their place, but carve a different path across the way and trail off, not to be repeated. I could sit here all day mesmerized by the flow and change to which each drop testifies. It's almost as if the sky is crying. Logically I know what is happening, but for whatever reason, I just want to stare, thinking on all of the tears I have shed. The raindrops make no excuse for and have to reason to explain why they fall—they just do. So beautifully they do. It is raining right this moment, and I hadn't an idea it was forecasted.

There are not too many people I encounter who say they never cry, but when I do, I am almost absolutely certain they can read the surprise on my face. We are God's creation, are we not? Don't we know that if our bodies produce tears when we are sad or joyful, two opposing emotions, and our Father fashioned us in His image, the tears we experience are directly given to us by Him to shed? My tears bring me comfort and draw me closer to God because I know He sees each one and collects them unto Himself. In Psalm 56:8, David asks God to put his tears in *His* bottle. He is so good to us. He is a loving Father.

Crying releases the tension and pain that is deeply rooted in our emotions. After a really good cry, the soul feels relieved. Maybe a little tired, but relieved. I can't imagine going through life so tense and under pressure and not having a way to express myself and release my pain through my tears. Pride sometimes gets in the way. God took away our heart of stone and gave us a heart of flesh when we came to Him in a believer's faith in His Son. He knows very well what keeps us from releasing the tears He gave us. Trust me, it is better to let your tears flow. Our bodies cannot handle the unreleased pressure; it will somehow find a way to be expressed, whether we like it or not.

Tears of joy are just as beautiful. Joyful tears flow uncontrollably too. Happiness, gratefulness, and contentment are triggers. Sometimes I am so overwhelmed by God's goodness and His creation displaying such beauty that my tears are instant and naturally begin to flow. Music about His glory makes me cry too. This reminds me of how there are times when the sun is shining brightly, but there is a rain shower gently falling all around. You look up toward the sky, and there is a not a cloud overhead, but still drops are sprinkling down. Oh, what magnificent beauty. Only God can do that. Just as a fresh rain cleanses the atmosphere and waters the ground for a fresh new growth, your tears cleanse your soul and nourish your heart, washing away the pain, releasing the pressure of the pain, and making ready your heart for healing. Please don't try to fight it. It is not symbolic of weakness. Quite the opposite is true. Your tears are a sure indication of a surrendered, transparent heart longing for cleansing and healing.

Our Lord Jesus, God in human flesh, shed tears when He walked on this earth. His loving and compassionate heart, over the condition of ours, led to His weeping. John 11:35 says, "Jesus wept." The next time you really want to cry, just let go. Your tears, given by God Himself, will be critical for your healing. You will experience such a release and have a feeling of calm and peace. It's so very worth it. It's okay because you have someone crying right along with you—your Father.

> *A time to weep, and a time to laugh; a time to mourn, and a time to dance.*

ECCLESIASTES 3:4

WEEPING WILLOW, WEEPING WIDOW

*W*illows—with their beautiful, strong limbs and leaves blowing in the wind—have always been one of my favorite trees. It occurred to me one morning, on my walk, while watching the willow by my neighborhood pond, that the graceful and slowing movements were also remnant characteristics of a weeping widow. Both stand with dignity and in beauty by the water's edge.

Closing my eyes, I awaited a current of wind to come along and breathe a breath of freshness on my limbs as a source of comfort. I longed to experience what the willow was experiencing. How can I identify with these two beauties? I myself am a weeping widow. In just a few short weeks, I will be standing by the water's edge of a massive ocean with my face to the wind. Being next to the water has always had a calming effect on me. I will wait, with eyes closed, for the wind to sweep across my face, as it chose to do that morning near the willow. A year and a half after losing my spouse to prostate cancer, I am still weeping over the loss that has left a large empty place in my heart.

That was once filled with comfort in knowing ...

Knowing there was a companion, a mate, an adviser, a strong shoulder to lean on, and a future of hope in sharing. When all of these things are stripped away, you start to wonder what could possibly be in store for a life single and alone. It has taken two years for me to able to check that little box that titles me a widow. I know I am not alone in this situation, and I am not wallowing in self-pity. I am reaching out to others who find themselves widowed, approaching seasons in life without their significant other.

I know my God, who has hidden me under His wings, will provide me with hope for the future. My prayer is that you will experience the same. Whether you are at the beginning of this journey, in the middle of this journey, or several years into it, our God will provide you with

His comfort. He designed the wind to blow gently as a reminder of His presence ever so near.

As you seek moments when you can plant your feet next to a body of water, open your arms wide, raise your face into the wind, close your eyes, and then let go. Feel the gentle comfort in your soul. Know God is with you. The Morning Light, and bright Morning Star, are always shining upon you. You are loved. Always remember that and hold onto THE hand of hope.

> *Now she who is a widow indeed and who has been*
> *left alone, has fixed her hope on God and continues*
> *in entreaties and prayers night and day.*

1 TIMOTHY 5:5 (NASB)

IT HURTS
TOO MUCH

I give. I do not want these memories anymore. It hurts too much to recall them and relive them over and over again. I have held on to them for so long. Painful memories of loss and feelings of abandonment have caused me to grow callous and leave me feeling numb. My family and friends know this fact well as I withdraw for fear of losing yet another meaningful soul. Memories will go with me wherever I go. They are mine forever in my mind and forever in my heart. Just like rushing to a destination for emotional release in hoping my circumstances will not follow me. Behold, they are there to greet me as I arrive. So I give. I let go and let God.

Here I am at yet another stage of grief. A chapter in my life is about to come to a close. I have sold our family home and am in the process of packing, storing, and selling items that my daughters and I have decided we are ready to let go of three years after Harry's death. This home was to be ours for years to come. We were to have more memories of laughter, not pain. Future sons-in-law and future grandchildren were supposed to run through these halls and sit at these dining tables. We planned to pass it down to the next generation. Death has a cruel way of robbing us of our earthly plans and hopes. The time has come to rebuild and start again. So I give. I let go, and I let God.

Yes, I am a believer. As a woman of faith, I am very aware of what the Scriptures say about having hope, joy, and peace in all circumstances beyond human comprehension. Standing from a distance and looking down upon myself, as if having an out-of-body experience, I saw a woman who was afraid, doubtful, sorrowful, and without direction. I had all these feelings in my shower a week ago. Accepting defeat in trying to manage and juggle change, I lay down on my side and let the flow of water rush over me entirely. I cried out loud, "Father, I give. I can't do this anymore. It hurts too much to hang on." I was a woman who was numb. So I gave it to God and let go.

TERRI LYNN SCHMIDT

I choose to believe God heard me that day, and although He already knows what lies before me, He is rushing to my side to hold me and sustain me. He knows my pain, and I believe with all my heart He understands. He orchestrated the entire move and closing of my new home. As I study my devotions in silence each morning over my cup of coffee, I feel Him there. Birds chirp, the wind blows, butterflies flutter. And I know He is there. I am comforted with being held. He is my only comfort. I will remain with Him for the rest of my earthly life until I reach eternity. He promises He will never leave us nor forsake us. I am so grateful for His faithfulness. My prayer is that you find your strength and comfort in the only One capable of the endeavor. Let go and let God.

> *"No man shall be able to stand before you all the days of your life; as I was with Moses, so I will be with you. I will not leave you nor forsake you."*

JOSHUA 1:5

THIS HOUSE

*S*elling a house you have grown to love and have lived in for many years can rip your heart into pieces. As you cry and glance back over your shoulder to take in every single memory, as if it were the very last breath you will ever take, you reach for the door and pull it closed ever so slowly and gently. Disturbing the lingering memories would be a dishonor. Instantly, that tight pain in your chest grows deeper as a lump forms in your throat. The thought of moving forward and never looking back consumes your entire existence. Here come the dry heaves. Tears are unstoppable, uncontrollable, and flowing in a steady stream.

Finding myself a widow, single mom, and empty nester—all at the same time—wasn't exactly where I thought I would be in this stage of life. Entertaining the thought of downsizing my home has aroused emotions within me I didn't even know existed. I will be downsizing from the home my husband and I built eighteen years ago.

In this house doorways were marked with each new growth spurt. Permanent marker from childhood drawings stained the carpet. Fingerprints were painted, framed, and put on display. Pictures and heirlooms were showcased as signs of love, devotion, and gratitude.

Holes left by push pins still show evidence of the place way up high where a Happy Birthday banner once hung. There's a tear in the rug where many a golf swing was practiced, and a dent in the wall marks the spot where that golf club got loose and went flying.

In *this house* we fought and rebelled, we cried and we yelled. In *this house* we lied and we tried, we shared and we remained silent. We slept and we prayed, we took and we gave. We hid and embraced, we walked and we raced through sun, rain, sleet and snow. Here love was made and prayers were prayed.

> *In this house we laughed and we cried,*
> *we lived and … we died.*

In *this house* God lived. I am so grateful He did, because we surely need Him now. Wherever you are in your house, stop a moment and be grateful for the roof over your head, shelter from the storm, and memories that have been lived.

> *"In my Father's house are many mansions: if it were not so, I would have told you. I go to prepare a place for you. And if I go and prepare a place for you, I will come again, and receive you unto myself; that where I am, there ye may be also."*

> JOHN 14:2–3 (KJV)

IDENTITY

Wait a minute.
I am Harry Maxson Schmidt's wife.
That is who I am!

What an amazing title to have. I based every bit of who I was, what I stood for, and where I belonged upon my husband's reputation. When Harry went to heaven, I began asking myself where I fit in. I also started questioning my abilities to communicate effectively because the passing of a loved one can silence you, giving you the feeling of having the wind knocked out of you with a punch to the stomach. I have friends and business associates who are married; some are also empty nesters. Now that the one person who defined my identity, Harry, was no longer in my life, I began asking myself, who is Terri?

Why do we align ourselves and associate with successful people for our identities? We love to mention the names and accomplishments of our acquaintances to gain respect and importance in the eyes of the listener. If we associate and communicate with people of influence, then we must be important too, right? We name-drop. We all do it. But why? I believe it is because we desperately want to feel important and respected. I had attached myself to my husband's reputation. His drag racing title as a Quarter Mile Legend made me feel important. Die-cast cars bore his name. Articles and newsflashes hit the internet in the racing world the moment of his passing. Here was the problem: It was his reputation and not mine.

The identities that we seek are within ourselves, not in another person. Even the very best of friends and loved ones cannot fill this void. We must do our own soul-searching to discover who we really are. Studying the Scriptures and knowing who we belong to helps mold our identities into what we become. We are children of God. Period.

I know that I carry an important name. More importantly, I know whose name I carry outside of my marriage now as a widow.

TERRI LYNN SCHMIDT

The Spirit Himself bears witness with our spirit that we are children of God. And if children then heirs—heirs of God and joint heirs with Christ, if indeed we suffer with Him, that we may also be glorified together.

ROMANS 8:16–17

A GOOD LIFE

*R*aise your hand if you do all of your thinking, crying, singing, or praying in the shower. The shower is where God gives me inspiration to write, and I can hardly wait to hop out and begin writing my thoughts as fast as my hand can keep up with my mind. I do not want to forget or miss sharing what was placed on my heart.

The day I came home to shower after visiting my husband in the hospital and learning he only had days to live, it was through tears that God gave me the title "A Good Life." Those three words can be found on T-shirts, baseball caps, and even jammies in sporting goods stores. We each have our own definition of what that small but powerful little statement means to us. If it's ok with you, I would like to go first in sharing mine.

My family has glided through the waters of the Amazon River in a river boat and hiked the National Park trails of the Rocky Mountains, Sequoia, Yellowstone, and Mount Rushmore. We have ridden in hot-air balloons over lush green and mountainous terrains of Southern California, gone white-water rafting through the Arkansas River in Colorado, and navigated the steep rock formations of Moab in a Jeep. Helicopter rides over New York City, the volcanoes of Hawaii, and the grizzlies of Glacier National Park were spectacular. Cruising through the locks of the Panama Canal and motor coach RVing across the entire western, midwestern, and southern United States offered sights we will forever remember. A favorite memory was of a baby Paint Horse running along the fence line in Wyoming, trying to keep up as we were driving by.

Some of you may look at this list and say that this could be considered an extreme bucket list. I think in some ways you are right. *Smile*. I have never looked at the list that way until now. I look at it as time invested in family and friends. Memories created to carry us through happy and sad moments of our lifetime. Time is something you cannot give enough of or ever get back.

A "good life" also consists of forgiving others when needed, going the extra mile to express a compliment when it is obviously deserved, and letting others have the upper hand when you know they are right. It's about showing respect to the elderly, protecting the innocent, and serving others with your life as much as is within your power. Lastly, it means apologizing when you know you are wrong and doing "the *next* right thing," as Harry Schmidt would say.

I have been crucified with Christ; it is no longer I who live, but Christ lives in me; and the life which I now live in the flesh I live by faith in the Son of God, who loved me and gave Himself for me.

GALATIANS 2:20

SOLITUDE

*L*isten. Did you hear that? What did *you* hear? Sometimes I hear ... well, crickets. Meaning silence. Or, when in Honduras, I hear the cock-a-doodle-doo of roosters near and then afar. The silence of solitude can be very much needed during a time of personal reflection. Eliminating additional busyness in our life can reawaken our senses, giving us a keen awareness of what is really going on around us.

On my walk last week, I watched two young squirrels in a playful high-speed chase around a large oak tree and two mallards dipping and flapping their wings after bathing in a pond. A cute duckling stretched a hind leg after standing from his brace during a time of rest. Leaves are beginning to fall from the trees in the afternoon breeze. All of this is happening during the daylight hours, enhancing our enjoyment of solitude. Otherwise, I may have walked right by them without taking notice. What happens when the sun begins to set and nighttime falls?

Nighttime brings to life a new meaning to solitude. The moon shines, and stars twinkle. Shadows dance, lights dim, critters slumber—everything is still. We are still. The world is at rest. We are at rest. We say not a sound with our eyes wide open. Time to breathe in solitude with our hearts open as well. **Solitude:** *The state or situation of being alone. Without other's help or participation; single-handed.*

Snuggling with my teddy bear, I am reminded that loneliness can be experienced even if you are with a large group of people. I can recall feeling that way for many months after Harry died. There were times I would rush home just to get alone to cry. Daytime became very long, and I looked forward to being alone so I could grieve. Fighting back tears and keeping emotions at bay just to function in the world was exhausting. Nighttime became even more grueling.

Reflecting, I sought to understand where I was in my life. What was the purpose of the trials and tests I was going through, and what was I supposed to learn from them? *Speak, Lord, speak* was my prayer. In my solitude I sorted through, prayed through, and then slept through the night until ... the night faded away and dawn began to break. Daylight surfaced to a new beginning. It was time to venture out. God created us for community and designed us to be part of a fellowship. When you are ready, leave the darkness behind and run to the Light.

But Jesus often withdrew to lonely places and prayed.

LUKE 5:16 (NIV)

REFLECTION

*O*ne of the most relaxing activities I have ever found is watching the sunset through the blowing trees that line the green belt behind my home is. The sun bounces off the water of my swimming pool, sending a glistening of light back to me, warming my face. Looking way up high into the sky, I see birds darting about, chirping and swooping as if to say, *"another day is coming to an end"*. Even farther up past the birds, a jet leaves a long white trail across the blue sky. The sun reflects from the body of the plane as it makes its way far into the distance. I follow the plane with my eyes until it disappears from my view, continuing on to its destination.

My gaze slowly drifts back down to eye level, where the sun once again peeps through the tree branches. Something new is now taking place, and it captures my attention. The sun bounces off the water of my swimming pool, sending a glistening of light back to me, warming my face. I can feel the glow from the reflection surrounding and illuminating my entire body. I feel at peace. I close my eyes and then open them ever so slowly as I do not want to miss a single moment of pure brilliance. It is time to reflect.

Where does your mind drift as you reflect? Happy times? Sad times? Were there huge milestones of change? Successes or trials? I myself reflect back over the years of being a wife and a mother. I reflect upon all the incredible adventures we had as a family. Just like the sun, my heart is warm, full, and aglow. My soul is saturated with beautiful thoughts of compassion, love, and commitment. As I sit perched upon a ledge near my pool, with my legs tucked underneath my crossed arms, I remain very still. A peaceful feeling overtakes me, and I relax into the final moments of the sunset as it projects an orange glow on a few scattered clouds above.

Another Son that reflects light comes immediately into thinking. This particular Son reflects such light that all of heaven and earth cannot contain it. His light is so bright you have to shade your eyes from looking directly into it. Much like the sun, this Son brightens our day. There is one thing though that sets this Son apart from the other. This Son's light never diminishes or fades away into the darkness.

It is a continual light that can never burn out. It is constant. It is faithful to warm the soul. We can always count on it to light our path and show us the way. If we spend a lot of time basking in it, we find that *we* become the reflection of this Son. This ought to invite us to come forth to that place of seeking opportunities where we can escape for a moment to reflect. The Son is waiting to shine upon you!

My heart cries out, Father,
may my life be a reflection of your Son
and be a light for your people
in this world that is filled with darkness.

As in water face reflects face, So the heart of man
reflects man.

PROVERBS 27:19 (NASB)

PRAYER

*P*rayer changes everything. Out of the very depths of our souls, our hearts cry out. Unaware of what we are truly asking for from the motivation of desire and need, God already knows what we will ask before it is spoken. He knows what is best for us in correlation to the path He has set our feet upon. His answer, or waiting delta before His reply, can come quickly or span a lifetime. Waiting on the matter at hand takes patience and perseverance—something I must discipline myself to embrace as I wait.

Now, as an adult, I am reminded of how important prayer is in all areas of our lives and in those around us. I am certain that my prayers are extremely selfish and self-centered. But through these prayers, God laid something on my heart that urgently speaks at a deep level of pain, which resulted from being a child of divorce. This feeling of abandonment—deeply buried in my heart—is a protective mechanism I put into place that keeps me from sympathizing with others who are dealing with intense pain. A loss is a loss. Pain is pain. My family has experienced both: death and divorce. On the other hand, I take on the pain of others, but cannot reach out to support them.

What to do about revelations
God places on our hearts through prayer?

Pray.

Prayers to Our Father can break through walls, bring down strong-holds, cast out fears, and set us on a path to healing. Only through prayer can God access and initiate the healing of heart issues that need repair. There is nothing too large or awful about our lives that Our Lord cannot heal through prayer. The Scriptures teach us that through our circumstances, trials, and heartache, we are being poised to, in turn, help those who find themselves in the same predicament.

Pray, pray, and then pray some more.

I have stopped right this very moment to ask for healing from my brokenness on the matter of pain regarding abandonment. I pray for your broken heart as well. Not allowing my Heavenly Father to heal areas of my brokenness has hindered my sending cards, flowers, regards, and moments of being present to those who are hurting. Together we are all moving through this life and learning to remain steadfast in our faith and hope. Allow yourself to go through the pain, whatever it may be, and then allow God to heal you as only He can. Pray with a humble heart, making your requests known, then be patient. God will answer your prayers. He is faithful.

Rejoice always, pray without ceasing.

1 THESSALONIANS 5:16–17

BLUE

*A*m I Blue? Yes, I'm Blue. My favorite color is blue! My birthstone is blue. My dining room wall and kitchen island are blue! The lake I live on is blue out in the deeper waters. Last night as the sun was setting, blue persisted all the way up to total darkness in the space where the rolling hills meet the sky. I watched it while lounging near my blue outdoor patio cushions. There is a section in my closet where I hang jackets and dresses, all the color blue.

Doing a little research on colors, when I came to blue, it all made perfect sense. I have surrounded myself with blue because the color promotes healing and calmness. The article goes on to say that there being only one food that is primarily blue, the blueberry, subconsciously we do not focus our attention on eating. Crazy, I know! That's what they said, not me! I knew there were many reasons that blue is my favorite color, and now I know some of them.

Blue is also the word we use to describe our mood when we are down hearted. Melancholy is more of the mood, but blue we are. Actually, I can see how it all ties in together. I write today surrounded by beautiful blues I created in my home for tranquility, with not a desire to grab a morsel of food due to my melancholy, blue mood. Makes perfect sense. Sort of. But why on earth am I blue? Now THAT doesn't make sense at all. I really can't explain it, but yet it is still there.

I believe it is because there is a longing. A longing for a revelation. I have faith. I have trust. I believe. God speaks to me. Yet, mysteries abound. Mysteries of the known and the unknown. I believe in Heaven and I believe in Hell. They are both absolutely, positively real. I want to know things right now and yet I want time to stop moving forward so fast. I look forward to extremely happy times that are on my horizon penned on the calendar, but I don't want to calendar my life away by going from the date to date of the "looking forward to's".

Can that be acceptable today? To not feel guilty enjoying the beauties of life as they evolve? Sunsets? Rainy days? Meaningful music? Without an agenda? Without being tagged lazy? I want to look at the calendar and tell it, "You are not the boss of me!" The revelation I seek goes deeper beneath the surface. We are such a surface façade generation. How does our hair look? How does our dress look? How does our car and house look? How do our relationships look? How do our children look? How does our job look? How does our WORSHIP look? On and on we go comparing our lives with the reflection in the mirror. I want more than that. I want transparency.

So, back to the blue mood. I think after working through it, I have a better understanding. It makes me feel a little blue. This world is in a heap of trouble right now and it breaks my heart. Through prayer, I seek to be an instrument God can use. An empty vessel perfectly filled up and overflowing with love and compassion. Speaking love with truth and humility. Setting all jealousies aside and turning my life into the direction where I see God at work. If I spend quality and quantity of time with Him, He will fill me with His mission. With all that I am, I believe that completely.

Are you a little Blue? That's okay. You are normal and just like the rest of us. Your longing is real. God placed it there. Longing for the right things is the key. Check your motives and ask God to sift your heart. Ask Him to reveal the reasons behind your blue mood. He will do that for you because He loves you, His child, THAT much!

> *Why am I discouraged? Why is my heart so sad? I*
> *will put my hope in God! I will praise him again;*
> *my Savior and my God!*

PSALM 43:5
(NLT)

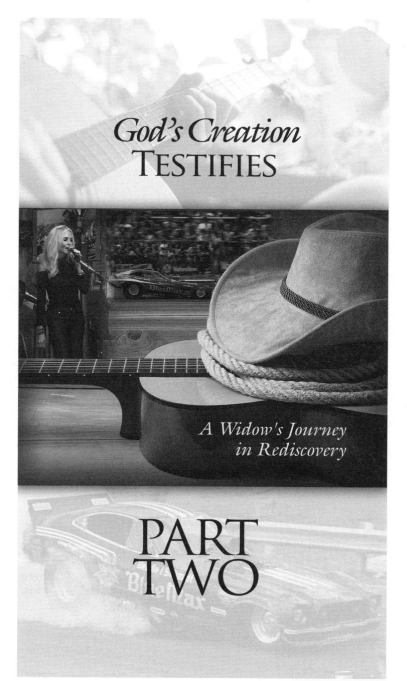

God's Creation
TESTIFIES

*A Widow's Journey
in Rediscovery*

PART
TWO

TERRI LYNN SCHMIDT

OCEANS

*H*onesty, whether I am near a pond or a lake, I love all bodies of water. But the ocean is a much different story! It is there that I feel my best.

Here's another bucket-list item: learn to scuba dive in order to see the "other" world God created. Beauty and life live in the depths of that vast spread of salt water. I am convinced I need to see it up close.

Something extraordinary takes place on or near the ocean. Not one thing can control it, redirect it, or stop it. That's humanly impossible for sure. Oceans have a mind of their own. Displays of emotion are parallel to human emotions. Raging waves give expression of anger. Glistening sunrays dancing on top reflect tranquility. Stillness in the water demonstrates calmness and peace. A storm passing over screams turmoil and strife. Crashing waves exhibit power and strength with boldness and confidence.

We approach the edge of these emotions with caution, allowing the foaming water to slowly tickle our toes in anticipation of chill or warmth. Deep down inside I can feel every emotion it mimics. Today I choose glistening sun, stillness, and crashing waves.

Usually when I am near the ocean, alone, I have ear buds in, listening to intimate selections of music that speak to my soul. The crescendo of the melody is so timely as the crashing waves tower in front of me. Awe. I stand in awe. Speechless. My heart calls out praises to the One who holds me near to His heart. People may be standing all around, but I am oblivious to their activity. My soul is refreshed by the reminder that the Creator's hand has intricately designed for this audience of one. Smiles, joy, laughter, and tears arise from the very depths of my soul as I am drawn to worship my Creator.

Yes, my Creator. He created the oceans and He created me. Scripture tells us to not trust in our emotions or feelings, for they can be tossed to and fro as the ocean waves. Bring them into captivity with the mind of Christ. We are to trust in Him solely by releasing every area of our lives into His care. Press into Him, and He will bring stillness and calm to you just as He commanded the ocean, "Peace, be still."

> *Who else has held the oceans in His hand? Who has measured off the heavens with His fingers? Who else knows the weight of the earth or has weighed the mountains and hills on a scale?*

> ISAIAH 40:12 (NLT)

Enchantment

G'day, mate!

The Land Down Under surely captured my heart. I am just a week within my return from a two-week adventure through Sydney, Brisbane, and the Sunshine and Gold Coasts. I rented a car and learned how to drive on the opposite side of the road with a steering wheel also on the opposite side. Challenging myself is the newest mind-set leading me into the next phase of my life. To my surprise, I caught on fairly quickly and really had a fantastic driving experience.

Back here in the States, I keep turning on the windshield wipers in my truck instead of the proper indicators and vice versa. Every single time I laugh out loud, as it reminds me of how quickly I actually caught on! It's good to be back in the good ole USA. But as far as Australia, I am blessed to have new family and friends that I will see again soon. There is simply so much more to explore.

Enchanting. That's the most profound word that comes to mind if I had to choose just one to summarize the feel of the land. If I may share with you while all is fresh in my memory, I will try to paint a picture of how God blessed me with opportunities to see His handiwork. As we learn with cameras in trying to capture a memory, the vibrant colors, sounds and smells are impossible to convey in a still shot. Yet I captured every fun and important moment.

Australia is a fairly young country—just over two hundred years old. Trees and flowers are lush, and a healthy green prevails this time of year as the Aussies approach their spring. Waterways, piers, and coves are full of transit taxiing, fleets of yachts, and monumental sailboats. From Sydney to Brisbane, the city architecture changed slightly, but the flavor was somewhat the same. Wonderful restaurants, cafés, and shops filled every corner along the footpath (sidewalk). Cities with towering buildings were definitely larger than I had anticipated. Uber, Pandora—two of my favorites were available and perfectly tuned in. I was a very happy American. All of the sights were just...lovely. Time came to move to the coasts, so car rental was in order. Luggage went into the boot (trunk) and off we went!

With a two-hour drive ahead of us, I climbed into the driver's seat and made my first immediate sharp left turn on the left side roadway. After a few deep breaths and prayers for angels to surround our car with God's safety, off we went. I was determined to implement this driving challenge. Thank heavens, we never experienced offensive Australian drivers. Instead, they were courteous and gracious, which helped ease my tension. Amazingly, we did not experience the speeding, aggressive, or darting drivers we find in the United States. Of course, our "Beware of Texans Driving" sign helped.

On the Sunshine Coast, surfers, ocean waves, and spirited dogs dashing along the shoreline, then plunging into the crashing waves, brought everything to life. Smaller quaint towns nearby touted oceanside dining and shopping boutiques galore. Pristine white sandy beaches, free of rocks or shells, made for an extremely tough departure. On the Gold Coast, we found yet another pristine white sandy beach. Amazingly, exquisite towering skyscrapers surrounded it. Enchanting indeed.

Above all sights and experiences, one tops my list of memories from my travel Down Under: trekking deep into the Enchanted Tamborine Mountain National Park to capture a magical moment at dusk. Traversing the forest of tall trees with massive divided trunks that were dripping with enormous vines of every kind and ferns growing off the sides, I can still hear the sounds and screams of critters I had never heard before. Waterfalls and butterflies, a chill in the air, along with chirps and songs of birds calling to each other as the darkness of night approached signaled it was time to enter the cave. There in the ceiling of the cave and surrounding rocks, glowworms lit up the night with their tiny bulbs. The finale to this journey through the mountainous terrain at nightfall was the appearance of fireflies. Magical!

All I can say is, "I am blessed. I am grateful. Thank you, Father, for opening my senses to enchantment in this beautiful land. I am honored to be a daughter of the King, whose creation is so magnificent!"

When DRAG RACING *met* COUNTRY MUSIC

> *Nor height, nor depth, nor any other creature, shall*
> *be able to separate us from the love of God, which is*
> *in Christ Jesus our Lord.*

ROMANS 8:39 (KJV)

TERRI LYNN SCHMIDT

THE COLOR GREEN

*R*ain, rain, go away, come again another day!

For one solid month in May, some of us were singing those lyrics as we witnessed record days and inches of rainfall in Texas. Memories of holding hands and trotting around in a circle with our siblings or best friends, singing this old song, as if one more repetition would summon a cease, brings a childlike smile to my face. Rain prevented us from being able to play outside in the yard and oh my, we were just not going to have that! Noses pressed to the window, and blowing hot breath steam to trace our initials, we waited patiently for the rain to come to an end so we could bounce outside and stomp our feet in the puddles along the edge of the yard. Rain hindered park visits and bicycle rides as our mothers proclaimed, "You will catch a cold if you go out in that rain!"

In my opinion there are two dominant colors in our world: green for the earth and blue for the sky. The clouds formed in the blue sky collect moisture and then release heavenly drops of water that in turn make for vibrant green trees, shrubs, and grasses. The stems of most plants and flowers are also green. Even though blue is my favorite color, green has certainly captured my attention. At the edge of the horizon, where blue and green meet, a perfect landscape is prepared—ready for the first brushstroke of the painter's masterpiece. Spring and summer promote the most vibrant colors of green we have throughout the year. Fall and winter have the ever-lasting greens. I am a spring baby, so maybe I should adopt green into my favorite color list!

Green is literally everywhere. We exercise the color in common clichés: He's green with envy. She has a green thumb. The grass is always greener on the other side. His eyes are as green as the day is long. Go green, recycle! If someone is nauseated, we announce they are green behind the gills. When giving someone permission to move forward with an action, we give them the green light. Performers tend to congregate in a green room before going onstage. We have a Green Giant representing beans, Jack climbing up a green bean stalk, as well as St. Patty's Day touting the little green leprechaun with a green four-leaf clover. Heck, even the Marvel gentle, raging giant—The Hulk—is green. Let's not forget about the almighty dollar. Wow, this color is versatile!

There is another green that represents peace and is found in a pasture, the one our Lord has provided where we find peace and rest. I have ventured out to our family ranch again and hoisted myself up through the sunroof to sit on top of my Rover. Perched on this ledge, I can scan across the green grasses, moss, and still water reflecting green from the trees. This is where I have found my inspiration for writing. I have come here to find peace and am overwhelmingly re-minded of the reason that my new favorite color is ... green.

> *The Lord is my shepherd; I shall not want. He makes me to lie down in green pastures; He leads me beside the still waters. He restores my soul; He leads me in the paths of righteousness for His name's sake.*

> PSALM 23:1–3

A FOUNTAIN

We all need refreshment, a chance to slow down. Our lives have become so busy and full of activity. If you are anything like me, sitting still for even thirty to forty minutes can be very challenging. Ever so often, we need a "fountain" experience. I am not referring to a drinking fountain, though it was at a drinking fountain that I met my husband. I am talking about a larger-than-life fountain that sprays high and wide in the middle of a large pond. A fountain that is magnificent, powerful, and strong.

While sitting near a fountain recently and walking by another, I pondered all the gifts they had to offer. First of all, the sound alone can quiet down your level of stress and anxiousness. I believe there is a strong connection to the ocean for a lot of people just for that reason. The sound is either constant or a changing surge force as the wind tosses it to and fro. If you happen to be too close to the fountain, you might catch a little spray of mist—a perfect rejuvenation to the face on a particularly hot day. When a ray of sunlight passes through the fountain spray, a beautiful rainbow appears. As the spray of water ascends and descends from the fountain and lands back into the body of water, a ripple effect is created.

Our attitudes and actions can create a ripple effect in the same manner. We are just like the fountain. We can reflect upon and rejuvenate another person in a positive way. All of us can spray a refreshing mist and add color to others' lives as well. At the time of completing this writing, I am in sunny and dry Tempe, Arizona. I have just finished climbing three flights of stairs about six times, moving my daughter out of her dorm for the summer so she could attend a daytrip to Sonoma with sorority sisters. Later I will have a fountain experience at the spa that will replenish my body. To replenish my soul and cool down from the heat, I will go to "THE" Fountain.

> *"I will open rivers in desolate heights, and fountains*
> *in the midst of the valleys; I will make the wilderness*
> *a pool of water, and the dry land springs of water."*

SISAIAH 41:18

TERRI LYNN SCHMIDT

CLOUDS

luffy white clouds float by from this view in the airplane. Stacked up below me, they drift by quickly overhead in a much thinner layer. I've got my nose pressed to the window as close as I can get to watch the show that I have been so blessed to witness. I have always been fascinated with clouds. They have many purposes and tell stories of their own.

As children we looked at clouds with imagination. Shapes of animals were pointed out. As we grew older, we started noticing symbols, and sometimes we could even make words out of them. By plane of course. When we were children, we were told that when our loved ones went to heaven, they would grow wings and hop around from one cloud to another—a world view of heaven. Of course, as adults we know better because the Scriptures are very clear. Many paintings have portrayed tiny cherubim with wings sitting on puffy whites strumming instruments.

Clouds actually do have a purpose outside of entertaining us with their beauty. White clouds transform into very dark ones as a storm begins to brew. After collecting moisture, they burst forth with rain that nourishes our land and fills our lakes. They are symbolic of a storm, and we speak often about either entering into one, being right in the middle of one, or getting through to the other side. On bright sunny days, we pray for a cloud to come and protect us from the burning rays of sunshine. We welcome the sweet, cool relief a cloud provides as it protects us with cover.

My family and closest friends have heard me say many times, "Keep your chin up and keep looking towards the clouds instead of looking down and focusing on the ground." Clouds give us a sense of calm and realization that this world and the Creator of this world are much bigger than we are. Something about how the clouds turn many colors during a sunset—burnt orange, yellow, and flaming red—surely can take your breath away!

If you have found yourself right in the middle of a storm brewing in the dark clouds, hang on. This too shall pass with time. There is a silver lining to every cloud, even if your situation is excruciatingly painful. If you are sitting on a mountaintop, watching a beautiful sunset light up the clouds with an array of colors, consider yourself blessed. You have weathered the storm. Be watchful, be hopeful, and continue to search every cloud expectantly. The Son of Man ascended into the clouds, and He will also appear again in the clouds. What a sight that will be to behold.

> *Now when He had spoken these things, while they watched, He was taken up, and a cloud received Him out of their sight. ... "This same Jesus who was taken up from you into heaven, will so come in like manner as you saw Him go into heaven."*
>
> ACTS 1:9, 11

FIELDS
OF WHEAT

Saving Mr. Banks: a must-see movie. It triggered a lot of thoughts and emotions in all areas of my life. The movie is a beautiful reminder of how to live again with laughter and music. For everyone, the experience of the movie will be completely different. If you have seen it, you know exactly what I am referring to. Without giving the movie away, there is a scene where a young daughter is riding bareback on a horse through a wheat field with her father. She is happy and content. Her heart is full of joy and love. There is simply no other place she would rather be.

Today I put on my cowboy boots, jeans, and leathers, then drove to our family ranch in Aubrey with my dogs in tow just to sit in front of a wheat field. It's not very often I have the privilege of going to the actual location that inspires my writing. Believe me, this was worth the drive. Even though the fields have been cut, I can remember how they looked when the wheat was a couple of feet high during warm weather months. This is a massive field of wheat and where I have parked my posse of doggies.

Wheat fields serve many purposes. As they grow, they become a hiding place for critters. When they are cut, they become food for cattle and horses. Though they are trimmed very short right now in the winter months, they soon will start growing tall and swaying in the breeze again. How very tempting, indeed, to hop on a horse and charge through as fast as you can go. Just as the father and daughter did in the movie scene. You can almost hear the calls and the whispers to stroll on in and the invitation to brush your fingertips across the tops along the way.

For me, a woman of faith who has taken many trips to the mission field, the wheat field brings yet another field to mind: a field ready for harvest. The harvesting of souls. My field may be different than yours. Yours may be your home or your place of work. Whichever it represents, be sure to spend adequate and extensive amounts of time in it. The fields at harvest can bring much joy and love!

> *"Don't you have a saying, 'It's still four months*
> *until harvest'? I tell you, open your eyes and look at*
> *the fields! They are ripe for harvest."*

JOHN 4:35 (NIV)

FLOWERS

*S*niff. Ah... Flowers.

Making her grand entrance at a wedding, a beautiful bride-to-be glows as her trembling hands grip tightly to the arrangement she is carrying. Her bouquet has been specifically designed with her in mind. She has handpicked each blossom. With their aroma and message of hope, flowers also comfort the hearts of those who are mourning. They adorn a tabletop and are the life of the party for a celebration. A mother receives a fresh bouquet upon the arrival of her newborn. They cause love to bloom in the hearts of lovers struck by Cupid's bow. Flowers come in all shapes and sizes—pure beauty in the eyes of their beholder. Seasons, climates, and regions determine the varieties that can be found.

I have a tiny bud vase on my nightstand that holds the smallest of roses snipped from a bush just outside my front door. I especially enjoy the stage between bud and full bloom. The flower is transforming from conception on the branch into a display of exquisite majesty. Each petal is rich in color. Time is of the essence if we are to enjoy the healthy, vibrant flower. We have only a short window before they begin to wilt and wither.

How do you handle your flowers? I enjoy them as long as I possibly can before they begin their decline. Removing them from their stand and putting them away before they completely wither allows them to bow out with dignity. I want to remember them in their healthy, vibrant stage. On the other hand, if the flowers have a sentimental meaning, I will draw them from their water source and lay them aside to dry, ensuring they maintain their beautiful poise. Dried flowers will last for years in this state if treated with care.

In springtime flowers will be in full bloom, so "stop and smell the roses." Their fragrance, appearance, comforting effect, and graceful demeanor should award them the title of "Timeless Beauties."

TERRI LYNN SCHMIDT

He has made everything appropriate in its time.
Also, He has put eternity in their hearts, except that
no one can find out the work that God does from
beginning to end.

ECCLESIASTES 3:11

Pets

*W*hen I was younger, my prayer life included a list of every family pet we had ever owned. I could call them all out by name with my eyes closed and tiny hands folded: "God bless Sugar, Sergeant, Duke, Pierre, Dutchess, Johnny, Jo Jo, Fred and Ethel, Stinker, Scamper" and so on and so on. Our family loved on cats, dogs, birds, gerbils, a goat, ducks, and even a raccoon. Not in that order or all at the same time, thank heavens! Well, maybe a few.

One summer a swarm of bees landed on the side of our home, trying to take up residence. A professional bee catcher had to come out and collect them for removal. I suppose they received word that our family took in all sorts of critters. We had ducks that swam in our bathtub or kiddy pool outside until we could find a new owner to adopt them.

If only our pets could talk to us, sharing their feelings and thoughts. Boy, would we be in for a surprise. They would make comments such as, *"You're leaving again?" "When are you going to feed me?" "I don't want to go into my crate!" "My tummy hurts." "My hips hurt." "My heart hurts when you are upset with me."* Still, they love us unconditionally with all they have. They keep our feet warm, save us from dangerous situations, and climb up into our laps when we need to be comforted.

I will always remember Scooter, my Brittany, lying parallel on my body to comfort me when I was crying during one of the saddest moments in my life. He stayed with me until my crying ceased. Pure love and devotion. Our homes would be quiet and lonely without them.

My Brittanys are ten years old today. I lovingly refer to them as "angels in disguise." They have beating hearts, breathe in the same air, and were also created by God. I wonder at times if our pets hear their Creator's voice in a different way than we do and respond accordingly. The very least we can do is to provide them with the love and care they deserve in return for all of the joy and laughter they bring to our lives.

TERRI LYNN SCHMIDT

Many of my friends have lost a deeply loved pet this year. A very painful experience indeed. Pets are very much a part of our families and play a large role in years of memories. In the Old Testament, Balaam's very faithful donkey spoke and asked him, "What have I done to make you hit me three times?" after the donkey had laid down upon seeing an angel of the Lord standing right in front of him. The Son of Man rode into Jerusalem on a donkey. David tended to the sheep. Animals were brought two by two into Noah's Ark. Obviously, God loved and used His animals for great purposes. In the order of creation, the animals were created right before God's greatest finale, man. I pray we show the same love, respect, and appreciation for our critters. Please protect God's precious creations.

> *God made all sorts of wild animals, livestock, and small animals, each able to produce offspring of the same kind. And God saw that it was good.*

GENESIS 1:25 (NLT)

FIRE

lames! They are red, orange, yellow, and blue in color. Fire is one of the four major elements that help us thrive and survive. Alongside water, wind, and earth, fire is an element we cannot live without. When fueled with a starter fuel and tossed with ash or pecan wood, the smell is so enticing and welcoming. We warm ourselves by it, stare into it, light the darkness with it, and cook delicious meals on it. Tonight, I am mesmerized by it. Watching the flames and feeling the warmth of them on my face is so calming.

I am almost positive that we have all toasted a marshmallow or two on a fire as well. The amount of crispiness the marshmallow on the stick or clothes hanger is, is all based upon the amount of time it's allowed to remain in the fire. The fire consumes the marshmallow and even though we extract it from the fire, a tiny spark consumes the little puffy ball and a new flame is ignited. If you blow on the flame, it will continue to burn until you completely put it out.

I just recently turned fifty, and oh my goodness! Seeing the flames that all those candles created was a little scary. Next time I'll be sure to keep a fire extinguisher close by. Smoke was abounding and causing much laughter—yet another example of the way fire makes its presence known. If you want to know just how important fire is, try starting one without a lighter. If someone has forgotten to bring the match to start the fire for a special occasion, they will search feverishly, high and low, until one is found.

The Native Americans used fire to communicate for help in distress or to send a message with smoke signals. The smoke created by the fire was fanned with purpose and precise timing to ensure the critical information was shared correctly. Sometimes life or death depended on it. Fires warmed them as they traveled from territory to new frontiers in snow-covered terrain. The fires also dried their water-soaked clothing. Without fire they could not possibly survive. I have studied this as a descendant of the Cherokee Nation. Again, this demonstrates how important fire is for survival.

TERRI LYNN SCHMIDT

Around Easter, I love to refer to my favorite Bible story surrounding the circumstances of Jesus' crucifixion and resurrection that includes a fire burning in the hearts of men. Jesus had just been crucified, buried, and resurrected on the third day. Two men were traveling on a road when He appeared to them and asked why they were so distraught and sad. They asked Him where He had been that He did not know about the events that had taken place. God concealed His identity as Jesus shared Scriptures with them, beginning with Moses leading to Himself. Our Lord has such a sense of humor and is so loving. After Jesus prayed, broke bread with them, and then vanished, the men's eyes were opened to who He was. The following Scripture says it all. Fire. All-consuming, burning in our hearts, and desperately needed.

> *They asked each other, "Were not our hearts burning while He talked with us on the road and opened the Scriptures to us?"*

LUKE 24:32 (NIV)

THE JOURNEY

*L*ife is a journey. Are you searching for a fabulous journey that will take you somewhere you have never been before? As we travel through this journey called life, it is not necessarily the end result that matters, but all that takes place along the way that can be the most thrilling. I have traveled through many states across our great nation with my family in a private motor coach. My eyes have seen some of the most breathtaking countryside along those journeys. One of the most memorable visuals I will always have while driving through Wyoming is of a baby paint horse running along the fence line, trying to keep up as we passed by on the highway.

From waterfalls in Glacier National Park to massive sequoia trees in Sequoia National Park to boulders and rushing rivers in beautiful Colorado, it's hard to comprehend the majesty of the landscape. From Mount Rushmore in South Dakota to flying by helicopter over volcanoes and steaming lava running into the ocean off the big island of Kona, Hawaii, to bucking and mating calls of elk in Yellowstone National Park, my heart could hardly take it all in. Old gold ore cars and mines with historic log cabins along lakes that can only be reached by foot were worth the trek. We drove across enormous rock formations by jeep in Moab and traveled out west across the desert, salt lands, and flat lands. These adventures are just a few of my journeys. Personally, I am in no way finished with my list. Next on the docket is skydiving.

As the navigator of our family travels, it was my responsibility to map out the next exits to keep us on the right path of our destinations. Being directionally challenged at times, I once lead us down a wrong road. We ended up in a residential neighborhood in our 48-ft. motorhome with a Tahoe in tow. With a rig that large in length, it is impossible to back up and make a U-turn. There is always the possibility of jackknifing and causing damage to the tow vehicle. The entire street came out to watch us unhook the truck, reposition the coach, turn around, and head back in the right direction. Boy, oh boy, was my husband frustrated and embarrassed. I went into hiding shortly after that. That one time our journey had come to a dead end. For only twenty minutes or so, but I was officially banned from Mapsco!

I would never trade our adventures for all the money or success in the world. If you need a way to clear your mind, refresh, start anew, and want to experience God's gorgeous creation, get in an RV and go. You will be grateful you did! After Harry's death to cancer, I will hold near to my heart every single memory of our family's travels together. Remember, the journey of life takes place in the space of the dash that represents the beginning of life and the end. What do you want your dash to speak to all who knew you? I want mine to say, *She lived life to the fullest, loved deeply, and never took her life journey for granted.*

> *Let all the earth fear the Lord; let all the inhabitants of the world stand in awe of Him. For He spoke, and it was done; He commanded, and it stood fast.*

> PSALM 33:8–9

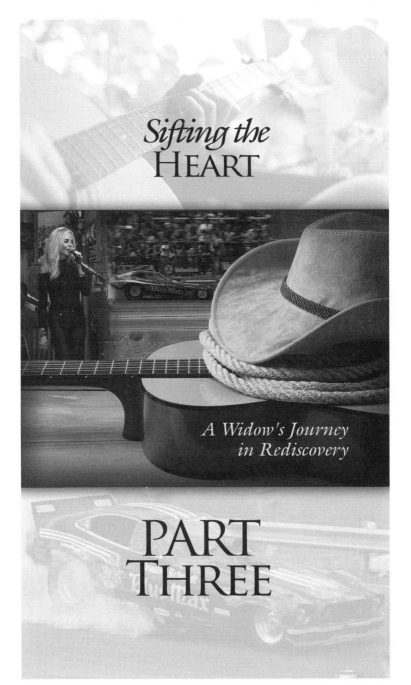

Sifting the
HEART

*A Widow's Journey
in Rediscovery*

PART
THREE

TERRI LYNN SCHMIDT

WALLS

I love the drive through the streets in my new neighborhood. Massive stone walls line the drive around every corner. There is not a deficit of stone in the Austin area. Suppliers are almost on every major intersection along the highways. An abundant supply makes for gorgeous stone walls throughout most of the newly developed areas. Meandering through, I began to recognize the importance of walls in supporting the construction of new homes and buildings. Drifting deeper into the thought of walls and how they are much needed, I considered all the different types of walls and what purpose they serve.

At this moment I am sitting in Breckenridge, Colorado, directly down the way from the cabin our family once owned. In the beginning stages of restructuring the lot where we would build the cabin, we desperately needed a new retaining wall to support the land from sliding down into the Swan River. The hoops we had to jump through to receive approval on the wall were very trying. After a two-year wait, we were given permission to move forward but were not allowed to remove or displace the large rocks along the edge of the river. A concrete wall was erected with large river stones to conceal most of the concrete. The wall served its purpose.

Walls provide solid foundations as well as privacy and protection. Centuries ago, walls were designed and built for castles, forts, and cities to keep the Enemy out. Office buildings have permanent walls and then within those walls, temporary walls to provide even a more private space for individuals. These walls are tangible and can be seen. Then there are those that cannot be seen. Intangible walls. I am referring to the ones we build around our hearts. These walls are much harder to destroy and tear down. They are hidden and not easily penetrated.

Heart walls, as I will refer to them, are erected to protect us from much more than those of stone. Building these walls can turn our hearts into a type of stone that *can* be seen with our eyes. We alone are responsible for these walls we have allowed to be built. If heart walls have been in place for quite some time, they are much harder to cast down. We have placed them there for a reason. We believe hiding behind them protects us from further harm, but our hiding only makes them thicker, taller, and stronger.

Walls that we build around our hearts are the direct result of substantial emotional wounding—blocks of hurt, anger, pain, abandonment, separation from loved ones, circumstances beyond our control, and even death. Unforgiveness creates a huge wall that begins to distance us as we slip into the fogginess of "I just don't care" protection mode. Stone. This "I don't care anymore" mode creates selfishness and a falsehood. Masks of pretending. Soon our hearts are as hard as the rock we use to build tangible walls. Unlike healthy boundaries, these walls cause separation. Separation from the ones we desperately love.

If we allow God to break through and tear down these walls, just as He helped the Israelites do in Jericho, we can have victory over our emotional walls. There is no wall too thick, too tall, or too fortified that our God can't tear down. The tiniest crack within the structure can cause an entire wall to come tumbling down. Allow Him to place the chisel into that penetrable area and strike with His healing hammer. Watch and rejoice as the walls come tumbling down. Victory! Amen.

When the trumpets sounded, the army shouted, and at the sound of the trumpet, when the men gave a loud shout, the wall collapsed; so everyone charged straight in, and they took the city.

JOSHUA 6:20

WISDOM

*W*ould you give up all you had in exchange for wisdom? If you were granted any wish that you wanted, would you request more money or longer life? Maybe you would follow King Solomon's request in asking for more understanding and discernment to lead his people. God granted him more wisdom because of his unselfish request. Solomon was wise to ask for more wisdom. He was known as one of the wisest men that ever lived! **Wisdom:** *Accumulated knowledge. The trait or ability to utilize or apply knowledge. To have common sense and insight.* At least this is what Siri told me when I asked her on my iPhone. I was wise enough to inquire!

In reality, knowledge equals wisdom. We have all been taught to believe that wisdom comes with age. The longer we live and the tougher the situations we encounter and get through to the other side, the wiser we become. The truth is, a young adult can be just as wise as an older adult. In 1 Timothy, Timothy started his ministry at nineteen. Yet, by the age of thirty, he had gained the respect of his older peers because of his growing in wisdom and maturity under the powerhouse leadership of the apostle Paul. Paul told him to let no one despise his youth.

My daughters, Hillary and Hailey, taught me how to use Facebook and Instagram. They also taught me how to tweet, text, and Face-Time chat all at the same time. I would have to say my daughters are wiser than me in the area of technology. I have seen young toddlers scan through movies at the dinner table on their parent's smart-phones and iPads.

What makes a person wise? A wise man can hear and increase learning at any age. My knowledge base in business started at nine-teen with a long span of Mommy Time in between until picking it up again at age forty-five. I do have the desire to acquire more knowl-edge and wisdom in growing my business. I am also wise enough to know the Gen Y group, twenty- and thirtysomethings, has a jump-start on me! The next time someone asks you, "If God granted you one wish what would that be?" Shout from the laptops, "Please grant me more wisdom!"

TERRI LYNN SCHMIDT

If any of you lack wisdom, let him ask of God, that giveth to all men liberally, and upbraideth not; and it shall be given him.

JAMES 1:5 (KJV)

TRUTH

*T*ruth can hurt, sting, and cut like a knife. We have all been on the receiving end of non-truth or half-truths. On the flip side of the coin, we have also been the ones dishing it out! Why, oh why, is it so hard to speak the truth? Closing my eyes and twisting my hair, I can recall several incidents in which I spoke half-truths. Yes, plural. Sometimes I outright lied! Shaking my head, I realize that confession and repentance are in order during my quiet time.

Many reasons or excuses keep us from speaking truth in any given situation: fear, resentment, envy, jealousy, and the granddaddy of them all—pride. Sometimes we speak half-truths in the name of that powerful four-letter word we all embrace... love. It's sad but *true*, if the truth be known. Would you like to know a fascinating concomitant regarding truth? It can set you free!

As believers, we proclaim God's Word is infallible and 100 percent truth. We know this because of the Scriptures based upon 2 Timothy 3:16–17 that tell us so: "*All Scripture is given by inspiration of God,* and is profitable for doctrine, for reproof, for correction, for instruction in righteousness, that the man of God may be complete, thoroughly equipped for every good work" (emphasis mine).

If we think back to the colorful Bible stories we learn as young children, they seem so far-fetched because of mind-boggling twists, turns, outcomes, and "only a miracle from God could do that" truth. Yet these stories are true because God's Word says it is true! Let's take a few examples from the Old Testament: Jonah and the great fish, Sampson's strength associated with his long hair, Daniel in the lion's den, God parting the Red Sea, trumpets and shouts breaking down Jericho's walls, and God carving the Ten Commandments on stone tablets.

Let's circle back around to the ninth commandment of those ten, where God makes it very clear how *He* feels about the truth: "You shall not bear false witness against your neighbor." This particular commandment is held up to this day in a court of law as we take the oath to "tell the whole truth and nothing but the truth"—with our hand on what? The Bible! If we know the Bible to be true and this command-ment tells us to speak the truth, how come we simply cannot master the truth? We are all sinners and fall short of the glory of God. God is perfect, and we are not.

Personally, I have learned that fear of loss is my underlying culprit. Loss of love, loss of friends or family, loss of position, loss of respect, loss of power, loss of trust, loss of reputation, or loss of everything at the same time. "Mercy, Father, mercy," is all I can say. Sadly, once a single lie is spoken, a multitude of other lies must come into play to protect and back up that one. Before we know it, we have a mountain of lies and we are walking in them and start believing them ourselves. If we are not careful, they will become like second nature to us and we cannot tell the difference from the truth or a lie. We break the ninth commandment. However, "if we confess our sins, He is faithful and just to forgive us our sins and to cleanse us from all unrighteousness" (1 John 1:9). Isn't that the most freeing Scripture there ever was?

Truth is powerful, and truth is freeing! Secrets must go. A guilty con-science must go. Fear must go. Start breaking down that mountain of lies until you get to the initial root. Breathe life into that falseness and make it truth, and then here is the beauty: Joy and freedom are found in speaking the truth!

> *"And you shall know the truth, and the truth shall make you free."*
>
> JOHN 8:32

MOTIVES

"Search me, O God, and know my heart; test my thoughts. Point out anything you find in me that makes you sad and lead me along the path of everlasting life" (Psalm 139:23–24, my paraphrase).

Amen. Time and time again, I have said this verse out loud. I know that God is the only one who knows a man's heart wholly and completely. He knows if we are conducting our actions from a pure heart. Even when we think we are acting out of a pure motive, Scripture again tells us that "the heart is deceitful above all things, and desperately wicked; who can know it?" (Jeremiah 17:9). So how do we know for certain we have true motives in our actions? We must examine ourselves.

Taking a good hard look within is never easy. This means that you have to take your focus and eyes off others and their faults and redirect that focus to examine only yourself. Honestly, it is so much easier to find fault in others—and complain, gossip, and crucify them for all wrongdoing—than it is to be diligent in examining ourselves to correct character flaws and actions that are not conducive to being a person of integrity. I myself have to make a concentrated effort to redirect my focus from the faults of another to my own actions—"bringing every thought into captivity to the obedience of Christ" (2 Corinthians 10:5). This process takes discipline and practice. It isn't easy, but with God's help, we can examine ourselves. As 2 Corinthians 13:5 says, "Examine yourselves as to whether you are in the faith. Test yourselves. Do you not know yourselves, that Jesus Christ is in you?—unless indeed you are disqualified."

What does all of this have to do with our motives? Every thought and every action we allow to remain in our minds without examining or aligning it with God's word will cause us to act out with impure motives. Humility is very important here, as pride will keep us from acknowledging and confessing our ugly motives. Sometimes we are consciously aware of our motives; other times we are not. God knows them both. We can't trick Him nor convince Him that our motives are pure. Rest assured, He *will* let us know! Examining ourselves is critical.

TERRI LYNN SCHMIDT

Me, I know that all too well.

Let's now examine ourselves. Are we jealous of others' successes? Do we desire the downfall of a person who has wronged us? Do we beg for God to avenge us? Do we see a speck in our brother's eye when we have a log in our own? Do we compare our blessings to others and become resentful? Do we sulk as others are promoted and recognized?

If we answered yes to any of these questions, it is time to stop and examine ourselves. Comparing ourselves to other people will only steal our joy. We are all on different paths in seasons of time. The mind is a battlefield, and the spirit is always at war with the flesh. Until the return of Christ, we will be in an all-out, full-blown battle.

Please remember, I desire to affirm that you are never alone. Ever. We are all doing life together, and though the Enemy is on the prowl to destroy, good will *always* win over evil, to the glory of God, even if we can't see or understand it now. How do I know? The Holy Scriptures, the Bible, tell me so.

> *Let nothing be done through selfish ambition or con-*
> *ceit, but in lowliness of mind let each esteem others as*
> *better than himself. Let each of you look out not only*
> *for his own interests, but also for the interests of others.*

PHILIPPIANS 2:3–4

SELF-CONTROL

I have studied Galatians, but I saw it in a brand-new light after having this conversation with God:

ME:
Father, please tell me, What I am missing?

GOD:
Self-control.

ME:
Wait a minute. Isn't that one of the Fruits of the Spirit?

GOD:
Yes, go back to Galatians and you will find it there.

I went there and found even more than I bargained for. I have always concentrated on the Fruits of the Spirit, and we all love to quote Galatians 5:22–23, but this time the passage starting at verse 16 brought a stark new revelation. I knew that our spirit is constantly at war with our flesh; however, I realized that *everything* our flesh succumbs to hangs in the balance of self-control or the lack thereof.

Self-control is pretty powerful. It's interesting how it is the last of the Fruits listed. Actually, if we could heavily rely upon it, our hearts, minds, bodies, and souls would be protected. Without controlling ourselves, we fall prey to overspending, overindulging, saying things we regret, acting on impulse, digging ourselves into a really deep hole, having one too many glasses of wine, and a multitude of heart issues. A person without self-control is a disaster waiting to happen. Destruction and devastation follow them wherever they go, and they leave a trail of brokenness in their path. Our world would be in shambles if government leaders had no self-control.

Expressions like "take a step back," "take a deep breath," "take a time-out," and "stop and think before you act" are all helpful in maintaining control of our actions. It's scary to think of how we would treat each other without self-control. Chaos would not even begin to describe the way of the world. I am thankful for that "Fruit" word. I have had to call upon it a million times in my fifty-two years. I would more than likely be writing to you from a prison cell if I acted upon all my impulses. I am thankful to identify the areas of self-control that I need to work on in my personal life. I hope a few of you have identified yours as well.

Our Lord demonstrated self-control in Gethsemane when He prayed, "Nevertheless not My will, but Yours, be done" (Luke 22:42). He marched straight into His destiny, knowing very well what was about to take place. His flesh had cried out for the cup to pass Him by, but He knew His Father's plan. He could have given way to His flesh and mankind would have been doomed for eternity. Instead, He gripped hold of self-control. He was mocked, beaten, scourged, stripped, spat upon, nailed to a cross by His hands and feet, and then crucified. He endured all displaying ... self-control.

We are like Jesus' disciples. Without self-control, we deny that we know Him. We run and hide from Him. We scatter. We blaspheme His name, abuse the gifts He gives us, and turn our backs on Him by satisfying the desires of our flesh. Oh, how I need self-control. The good news? Even though Jesus died on that cross, He came back to life on the third day, just as He had spoken and His Father had promised. He died so the Spirit can live inside us upon our confession of belief, trust, and faith in Him. There we find the power to choose self-control. Let's follow His example.

> But the Fruit of the Spirit is love, joy, peace, longsuf-
> fering, kindness, goodness, faithfulness, gentleness,
> self-control. Against such there is no law.

> GALATIANS 5:22–23

PEACE

*S*halom! I have returned from Israel after taking my daughters on a tour to the Holy Land with a large group and our church Pastor. After a day of touring and learning and following the foot paths of Jesus, my girls and I rested in our hotel room in Tel Aviv and I drifted off in thought of the true meaning of peace. Did you see Israel in the news recently when they had snowfall? Simply amazing! As I woke this morning back in Dallas, to a tender snowfall, I am reminded of how snow can be light, graceful, quiet, and... peaceful.

Do you have PEACE? Peace that surpasses all understanding? While strolling through the Synagogue in Capernaum I tried to imagine all that took place within those remaining walls. Some of the original wall is still standing with newer stones, from the Fourth Century A.D., built on top of the older. The walls are white stone and aging with weather and time. What took place inside those walls is forever ageless, profound, and everlasting. Our earthly bodies are decaying until we exchange it one day for a Heavenly body that will remain throughout eternity, and also... forever ageless. Just like the gatherings inside the Synagogue were truly meaningful, what lies inside of us is what matters.

How are you taking care of what is going on inside of you? Are you searching for peace? Peace can calm the anxious soul. Peace can fill your heart with joy even if you cannot forge a smile. Peace can restore your life after a heartbreaking situation. There is rest to be found in Peace. The knowledge that *Someone* greater is watching over us and guiding our footsteps, creates a peace that carries us until we are able to walk again. Have you found Peace? Standing in the Synagogue I found Peace. I knew I was standing on the same ground where the Prince of Peace once stood. Seek hard after Peace and you will find that what transpires inside will make its way to be revealed on the outside!

*Now may the Lord of peace Himself give you peace
always in every way. The Lord be with you all.*

2 THESSALONIANS 3:16:

TERRI LYNN SCHMIDT

REJECT, CONFESS, AND LEAVE IT

*C*ircumstances, feelings, heartache, unfulfilled dreams, or even thoughts can bring us much pain. I promise you if you are human, you are experiencing an *it* in your life that you would give anything to rid yourself of. Maybe it is regret over a situation that you intentionally walked into, knowing what the outcome would be. You probably were even warned to approach with caution.

As a woman, I know all too well how emotions can play a huge role in decision-making over the *it* we have in our lives. I hope I am not out on a limb here all by myself. I have a feeling I'm not. I will speak only for myself, but at times I can be a really emotional person! Making decisions based on facts and not fiction can be a little challenging for me, especially during times when I am really busy with a lot of projects on my plate.

What does it mean to actually reject, confess, and leave something? First of all, let's identify one thing that we need to take through this process. Let's use, for example, a thought that is negative, condemning, or hurtful. We tell ourselves that we can never be good enough. There is no way we can measure up to everyone's expectations of us. When we fail at a task, we speak a lot of false claims and accusations over ourselves that we know are not the truth. These thoughts are all from the Enemy. The one who comes to kill, steal, and destroy our lives.

First, we must *reject* those thoughts as false claims. Next, we need to *confess* that we know what the real truth is to the One who is Truth. We may need to also confess a sinful thought pattern that has us in bondage. Last, *leave* it behind. Turn and move forward into the direction of the way, the truth, and the life. Take a few minutes and sit still to navigate through the process. You will experience a sense of freedom and a new beginning.

I know this is a strong subject. I am just sharing with you what was placed on my heart. I have grown to love my readers. I truly desire the best for each and every one of you who is hurting and struggling with matters of the heart. Brothers and sisters, be strong, bold, and courageous after you take yourself through the process. I am cheering you on!

> *If we confess our sins, He is faithful and righteous*
> *to forgive us our sins and to cleanse us from all*
> *unrighteousness.*

1 JOHN 1:9 (NASB)

BEING GRATEFUL

*S*itting here putting pencil to paper, I lift my head up from the covers that I am snuggled down in and stare at the words *Being Grateful.* Before I begin to write, I put my head back down and close my eyes and thank God for the blessings I am most grateful for in my life. Too many blessings to count.

GRATEFUL:
Affording comfort, feeling, or showing gratitude.

New babies, blooming flowers, beautiful sunsets, and fresh dew on the lawn can fill our hearts with gratefulness. As well as a beautiful marriage, a warm home, and a safe place to rest. Have you noticed though, how difficult it is to be grateful when things are not so beautiful or not so comforting? Being grateful during hardships is one of the hardest human traits to master. We start comparing ourselves to others and how they have been blessed. All of a sudden our blessings do not seem to measure up. It is easy to be grateful when things are going your way. Not so easy when they are not.

What happens when things are not going according to the plan you intended? Are you still able to say, "I am grateful"? When we take our eyes off what we are grateful for and gaze upon what we are lacking or hardships, we can become disheartened. Those times reveal what we are really made of. Listing below a few of the things that I am grateful for at this time in my life, I bet you can relate to at least one of them.

I have a roof over my head, a warm bed to rest my tired body, filtered water running through the faucet, a reliable vehicle for transportation, and food in my refrigerator. I live in a free country where I can pray openly with family and friends and a church that I can worship and seek encouragement from God. I have memories of family togetherness and bonding. I am grateful for all these things and to my Savior for sacrificing His life for me.

There are people living in third world countries who lack one or all of the items listed. I have been there. I have seen it for myself. The remarkable thing is that the people living in the small villages along the

TERRI LYNN SCHMIDT

Amazon River, if they do not have satellite, are not aware of the luxuries we experience here in America, and yet they are satisfied. They have discovered the character trait of being grateful for what they do have. We have the same capacity inside each of us if we will exercise it. Remembering and being thankful for your blessings makes for a very grateful heart.

You are my God, and I will give You thanks. You are
my God; I will exhalt You. Give thanks to the Lord,
for He is good; His faithful love endures forever.

PSALM 118:28-29 (HCSB)

T.R.U.S.T.

eturning from an eleven-day trip to Honduras in Central America, I have grown to love the country and its people. My first visit was back in 1989, performing for our troops through the US Department of Defense (DOD). This trip consisted of visiting and delivering supplies to the children at La Finca de Los Niños Children's Home and spending time building stronger relationships with my Honduran friends. Leaving the familiar surroundings of home and my family in the States to travel to Honduras, by myself for the first time since I started visiting the country, took a lot of T.R.U.S.T. on my part.

Trust is a universal heart issue and encompasses a multitude of areas. We have difficulties with trust in relationships, decisions, provisions, and our own insecurities. Relationships can hurt, decisions can be altered, provisions can instantly disappear, and we can experience fear and doubt of security when we are left alone or feel abandoned. Even though I had a difficult time leaving my country with the passing of my husband in April 2012, I had made a promise to the children at La Finca to return for a visit. It had been shared with me to not make promises to the children I could not keep. Their hearts had been deeply hurt by abandonment. I wanted them to *trust* my word. I chose to keep my word and boy, I am glad I did. Their trust and belief blessed my heart.

Have you been hurt deeply because you have placed a high level of trust in someone and they could not fulfill their promises? I have always had an issue with the matter of trust. Most of the time when I have trust issues, it is because I have allowed myself to become disappointed by a broken word or action, and I have not exercised forgiveness to move forward. As adults, we have the ability to learn how to exercise forgiveness. We forgive as we have been forgiven through grace. It is not an option. We have been forgiven, so we must forgive. Holding brokenness against someone causes bitterness and then it becomes an excuse to not trust again. *Trust* me, I know!

In reality, man is fallible. We are not perfect. There is only One who is. Because we are imperfect, we will fail, let others down, and will often times be led by our emotions instead of facts. Feelings are a beautiful thing, but not always to be trusted. Be careful not to place expectations upon others that you are not willing to place upon yourself. Do everything in your power to keep your word. Try not to make promises you know you cannot keep. Stand up and take responsibility for your actions or lack thereof. Forgive others for their shortcomings. The more you forgive unmet expectations, the more free you are to begin to trust again. My acronym for T.R.U.S.T.?

Total... Reliance... Under... Specific... Trials!

> *Trust in the Lord with all your heart, and lean not on your own understanding; in all your ways acknowledge Him, and He shall direct your paths.*

PROVERBS 3:5–6

PERFECTION

*W*hat an exquisite spa in Scottsdale, Arizona. Donna was about to administer a Thai massage, and we landed on the topic of perfection. I loved our conversation so much that I thanked her for the idea for a title for my column. We talked about how much we all strive to reach perfection in every area of our lives. We realized that even though it would be nice to be as close to perfect as possible, it is likely impossible in this imperfect world.

Why do we seek perfection? We are driven by the constant search for it and can never be completely satisfied until we have tried our hardest to obtain it. Whether we realize it or not, we expect it of ourselves, our family, and our friends. We want our marriages, relationships, bodies, jobs, and earthly possessions to be, well, perfect. It is no wonder that we become disillusioned and disheartened when we cannot obtain it.

PERFECTION:
Lacking nothing essential to be whole;
complete of its nature or kind;
to be without blemish or defect.

How is that working for you? Believe me, I am just as guilty. When I was a young adult and immature about relationships, I used to believe that if a relationship was not perfect, then it was just not meant to be. It took a very strong, mature man to show me otherwise. Once I was able to accept that relationships were not going to be perfect, I was able to move forward and look forward to future possibilities. My understanding began to stem from commitments and working on the relationship instead of dissatisfaction.

My daughters and I exercise at a CrossFit location to get a better handle on our health and strive to have stronger, more durable bodies. You better believe we desire to have bodies that are as perfect and healthy as possible. It is important to remain healthy as long as you possibly can. Our future generations depend upon that at some level. Even though we desire perfect bodies, we understand this human desire cannot be completely satisfied or obtained.

There is only One who is perfect and whole. One who is without blemish or defect. The spotless Lamb gives us His definition of perfection.

And He said to me. "My grace is sufficient for you, for My strength is made perfect in weakness." Therefore, most gladly I will rather boast in my infirmities, that the power of Christ may rest upon me. Therefore I take pleasure in infirmities, in reproaches, in needs, in persecutions, in distresses, for Christ's sake. For when I am weak, then I am strong.

2 CORINTHIANS 12:9–10

HOPE

*O*hope it rains tomorrow! I hope I make it to the airport on time! I hope when I go to bed I won't feel that pain in my back! I hope I won't fall wearing these high heels! I hope he makes it home safely! I hope they are careful driving in the snow! I hope they know how much I love them. I hope, I hope, I hope. Sound familiar? Our hopes of a better world and a better self are at an all-time high in these days and in days to come.

Are you hoping for a new job or for a new direction in life? Maybe a new love, a new baby, or a new home is at the top of your list. Maybe you just want a chance at a new beginning. The list goes on and on. Without hope, moving forward past heartaches and stressful situations would be close to impossible. Hope in a new tomorrow creates in us a desire to make the most of today with what we have been given. Even when it seems like all else fails, there is still a little glimmer of hope. We hold on to it for dear life.

Each of my daughters had challenges this past year that could have easily caused them to lose hope. I have asked each of them to share with you what hope means to them:

> **Hillary:** *Hope is the feeling of security. It is the moment you put all your trust in the Lord to help you. Hope is what helps you get through troubled times and helps you look forward to the great times.*

> **Hailey:** *Hope is having faith in God. Faith that He will watch over you and be in control when you feel like your world is falling apart. Hope is knowing the next day won't hurt like the day before.*

> **María José (my Honduran daughter):** *Hope, the reminder from God that no matter how hard our times are, He has prepared something much greater for our future, whether in heaven or earth. Hope reminds us to rest in Him.*

Are you living without hope? A sense of hopelessness can lead to a feeling of defeat. It is in our despair that it is most important for us to hold onto hope. God tells us that we can be confident in hoping in Him. He is with us, provides for us, and is always in control. Place your hope in Him.

> *"For I know the thoughts that I think toward you,*
> *says the Lord, thoughts of peace and not of evil, to*
> *give you a future and a hope."*

JEREMIAH 29:11

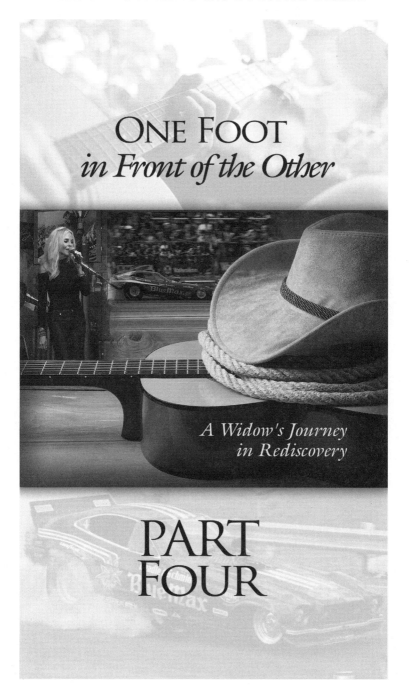

ONE FOOT
in Front of the Other

*A Widow's Journey
in Rediscovery*

PART
FOUR

TERRI LYNN SCHMIDT

BLANK PAGES

What is your life story? Everyone has one. Some are happy. Some are sad. Some are honest ... while others are made up. You may have been blessed with the opportunity to write your own story, while others have had theirs written for them. Our stories tell the tale of what makes us who we are and what we stand for. If someone has dictated your life story and you are not happy with the way it has been written, there is good news: You can rewrite and start anew.

A blank page is pure, white, and clean. A blank page is ready for tearstains, fingerprints, and thoughts that are poured over and poured out on. Close your eyes for a minute. Can you see pictures in your mind? Your life is being played out right before you. Your dreams, aspirations, and goals still predominate. They are still evident. For some reason, they just seem a little more out of reach or far-fetched than they used to be. Your life has not turned out the way you had originally planned. Do you dare rewrite and start anew?

Your blank page is ready. If you need a little inspiration, turn on your favorite song, grab your cup of coffee, sit in your favorite spot, and begin to write. Remember, life is a moving target, and we are not always prepared for what comes our way. One thing I have realized about our life stories is that they are constantly changing. We are going along and then all of the sudden—*bam!* Life takes us in a direction we had not planned. If you are willing, it is time to rewrite and start anew.

We find ourselves faced with a choice. We can choose to remain the same or we can make the necessary changes to move forward in a new direction. We have a choice between taking action versus taking a passive attitude of playing the victim—a decision must be made. Please trust me on this one. I have been at that crossroad myself many times. Years ago—I cannot really say when—I made the decision to refuse to play the victim. I stopped blame-shifting and allowed myself the privilege of writing the next chapter in my life. I chose to rewrite and start anew.

I wish I could read the stories you will write. I know they will be so amazing and interesting, full of life and intentional. They will have meaning and purpose. You will look back and discover the moment you decided to move past your current circumstances and take a different path at that crossroad. It will be the story of your choosing as much as it is up to you. Before you know it, you have rewritten and started anew!

> *"Sovereign Lord, I know that you have shown me only the beginning of the great and wonderful things you are going to do. There is no god in heaven or on earth who can do the mighty things that You have done!"*

> DEUTERONOMY 3:24 (GNT)

RESET

*T*imers on stopwatches have Reset buttons. Athletes use them all the time during training to monitor their progress: each jump, stroke, or the total distance. We can only guess how many times in the career of an athlete that the Reset button is pressed. In everyday life, we set timers to let us know when our treats have completely baked, color on our hair has set, or scheduled meetings have concluded. We even time silly things, like holding our breath under water. At the ding of that timer, the Reset button is pressed if we need more time or want to start all over.

I want to start over!

We press virtual Reset buttons in our minds when we reach a point of exasperation and have no idea in which direction to turn next. Take a deep breath, push your shoulders back, reach for that Reset button, and give it a hard push. Believe me, I have worn out my welcome by pressing it way too many times. I have made so many mistakes in making wise choices. Sometimes I have to reconsider my decisions and plead for a reset—especially when people are counting on me. Start over. This is where I must give myself grace and realize that I am normal and we *all* have moments when we are thankful for that little button.

Confessions made. Forgiveness granted.
Grace offered. Resets given.

No questions asked.

Our Father is the *master* of extending the "start over" option to His children. He understands that we are incapable of living a life that entails perfect decisions and actions. Through the gift of belief, trust, and faith in His Son, we have full access to His holy Reset button. Without it, we would all be condemned and deserve punishment for our wrong choices. I am eternally grateful as I approach the throne of grace humbly and stretch out my hand to gently press that button.

Remember, our God says He will never leave us or forsake us. And

TERRI LYNN SCHMIDT

He calls us to extend His grace and forgiveness to others. Sweet brother and sister, it's okay. Press that Reset button.

> *Seeing then that we have a great High Priest who has passed through the heavens, Jesus the Son of God, let us hold fast our confession. For we do not have a High Priest who cannot sympathize with our weaknesses, but was in all points tempted as we are, yet without sin. Let us therefore come boldly to the throne of grace, that we may obtain mercy and find grace to help in time of need.*
>
> HEBREWS 4:14–16

MOVING ON

LA, here she comes! It hasn't quite hit me yet. My youngest daughter has chosen to move to Los Angeles after graduating from college and *not* come back to Texas. Who am I to stop her from spreading her wings and soaring toward the visions of her dream? As part of an RVing family, she has traveled across the entire United States, save the East Coast. Lived in Colorado in the summers and California in the winters.

Travel is not new to her. Precisely what her dad and I intended to instill in our children. Well then … why does it hurt? Why am I offended she has chosen not to live near her family? My daughter has chosen to *move on*. On a more serious note, I truly am happy for her and excited to see where her vision takes her. I must accept her decision to move. But really? LA?

Painful as it may be, moving on requires change—change of scenery, change of surroundings, change of lifestyle, or change of circle of influence. Good heavens to Betsy … maybe it entails all of the above! Before we go into panic mode here, let's stop and be still. I share on this as a widow for four years. Therefore, change is neither foe nor friend when I am looking it straight in the eye. Always, there seems to be the word "drastic" attached to it.

Have I moved on and embraced the change of my scenery and surroundings? I believe mostly that I have.

Boy, did I ever fight it in the very beginning! I used to travel to destinations alone to run from change only to find that sneaky little verb has hopped into my luggage. Have I accepted the fact that Harry is not going to walk through the front door during the remainder of my life? I shall never again hear his voice or laughter on this side of heaven? Mostly I have. Yet, the pain still remains—a change forced upon me that I did not want to embrace. The Holy Spirit was the only person who walked me through it. He is the Comforter, and God Himself understands that level of pain.

TERRI LYNN SCHMIDT

Moving on does not mean you have to forget. Moving on does not mean you have to stop loving. Shame and guilt have no place in the moving-on process. God is in control and overseeing your circumstances the entire time. Take comfort and trust in Him, leaning not on your own understanding. Loved ones here on earth and in heaven are in His grip. There is no time line you have to adhere to. Take all the time you need. God's got this! Let's move on together. We are here because He wants us to continue to live.

In the early years of my daughter's schooling, I dressed as the biblical woman, Ruth, and enacted a memorized scene of her story for a grade level. I dressed the part and acted the part with props in hand. Ruth is a beautiful example of moving on. As a young widow, she chose to leave her homeland and follow her mother-in-law, also a widow, to Moab or wherever she traveled. Ruth's husband, Naomi's son, had died. Their circumstances had changed immensely and were completely beyond their control. Yet, God had a plan. He was always right in the middle and knew even the tiniest of details. Have courage in your moving on by standing on that knowledge, my friend. He has a plan and is also smack-dab in the midst of it all. Don't be afraid to move on.

> *But Ruth said, "Entreat me not to leave you, or to turn back from following you; For wherever you go, I will go; And wherever you lodge, I will lodge; Your people shall be my people, And your God, my God."*

RUTH 1:16

IF I FALL?

*F*alling down and scraping our knees hurts so bad. Yet, we stand up, dust ourselves off, and keep walking. Perhaps a bandage over our wound is required, but we just keep going, painful as each step may be. Our hearts have a few tears and scars from falls as well. Oh, they are so painful on the way down. We feel broken, which just like a broken bone, takes a little more time to heal. The positive here? Our Lord God is the ultimate Healer and knows about every one of our painful falls. Physical and emotional.

I have fallen many times in my fifty-two years of living. Some falls were due to my own negligence, while some were circumstantial. A telephone pole wire had the nerve to grab hold of my bike handle and wrestle me to the concrete, fracturing my elbow in my early forties! With my helmet down in determination to pick up speed, I never saw it coming, so you can imagine the initial surprise—and pain. While in Australia, I broke two of my toes on one foot when a chair fell over on them. More pain.

Would we ever choose a fall purposefully?

Well, yes, if you really think about it. We fall in love. We fall out of love. We fall into temptation. We fall for "it." We fall "head over heels." We fall flat on our faces over and over again. My personal opinion is in some cases we do have a choice. Remember the phrase, "If you don't stand for something, you will fall for anything"? This addresses all areas of our lives: faith, morals, integrity—literally everything.

I remember once during a CrossFit class being face-down on the rubber mat with my nose touching ground and my eyes staring at the black mass. I felt lifeless as I fought an overwhelming feeling of defeat and exhaustion from an emotional struggle from previous days. Overcome with deep emotion, I began to cry. Faced with a decision, I had two choices. Stay on the floor fallen, face-down wailing in tears or push myself back up from that burpee and stand to my feet.

I stood.

TERRI LYNN SCHMIDT

I am not patting myself on the back here for being strong enough to stand. It took every ounce of strength that I could muster to push myself up off that mat. You probably have had to do exactly the same. It takes true determination to press forward after a fall. Are we allowed a resting period after a fall? I believe so. Try not to stay there too long though, you might get a little too comfortable in the rest and the standing back up could involve slow motion.

In the resting we find healing, we find peace, we find strength, and we find God. He is in the midst of our fall. He understands the human struggles we all have and still He gives us His Word to guide us and encourage us. We can place all of our trust in Him and lean upon His strength until we are capable of standing again. What a merciful God we have and serve! Do not fear the fall. He is standing there to catch you when you do. You will stand back up again!

> *Be on your guard; stand firm in the faith; be courageous; be strong.*

> 1 CORINTHIANS 16:13 (NIV)

CONNECT THE DOTS

*P*encil on paper, we begin: 1 to 2 to 3 to 4 to 5 to 6 to 7 to 8 to 9 and 10. Curve 11 is next in our "connect the dots" picture. With great anticipation, we expectantly draw to the next line. We haven't seen the big picture yet—only a portion. Possibly, the next lines we draw will confirm our vision. If you are like me, you fervently scan the big picture, trying to figure out the image. I have also turned the page and began connecting new dots if I didn't like the current image surfacing. Sound familiar?

As I was preparing to speak to a group of women in Uganda, something occurred to me. Everything that had happened in my life led me to exactly this moment in time. Whether bad or good, happy or sad, everything was for a reason. Circumstances that led me to right here, right now; of being able to share my heart. My thoughts bounced back and forth from event to event, when I realized that each one had either built upon the other or was somehow related to the others. People included. Along my path of walking in faith, though not easy at times, God was always orchestrating the entire process. He never took His hand off me.

I wonder how many of us would actually stop for a moment and contemplate all the scenarios in our lives, then have a moment when we say out loud, "So *that's* why all of this has happened!" We seem so surprised and caught off guard by our discovery. Why are we so surprised? We prayed for it. We pleaded and begged for it. We denied it. We ran from it and even sabotaged it because we were scared of it. Yet we couldn't stop it. Then we come to the point of exclaiming, "Wow, no wonder!" Shocking, isn't it?

Our dots can be confusing when the plans we anticipated are not quite working out the way we thought they would. Believe me, there is a purpose for that as well. If we are smart, we will connect our dots in the order that is laid out before us and try not to skip a number, forging ahead skipping through the present. Our picture would be all jumbled up and unrecognizable in our frenzy to reach the outcome in haste. Oh, but don't worry. There is one person who will make sure we stay on the path to the next dot. He sees and knows the big picture. If we jump ahead, He is sure to rein us back in.

Hold up a minute! What if the next line obviously includes pain and heartache? Well, there is a purpose for that as well, though we may not see the big picture this side of heaven. Even if your pencil is shaking and your line to the next dot is a little crooked or bent in anxious nervousness, the next dot is awaiting your approach. No need to fear it or begrudgingly accept it, for it is serving a purpose.

I have looked upon all my dots and have seen God's mighty hand orchestrating it all as He reveals a portion of the whys. What about the other ones? He has yet to reveal them, and I am awaiting His timing in sharing. I have approached my next dot. At the moment I am not sure if it is number four or twenty-four, but I do have a smile on my face as I write. I smile because even through the uncertainties and heartache, coupled with excitement and anticipation, I know for a fact God is drawing my entire picture. There are no accidents with Him. That is my faith, my hope, and my future. I place my entire life in the Master's perfect plan.

> *And we know that God causes everything to work together for the good of those who love God and are called according to His purpose for them. For God knew his people in advance, and He chose them to become like His Son, so that His Son would be the firstborn among many brothers and sisters.*

> ROMANS 8:28–29 (NLT)

Weights

"Five sets of ten, at 90 percent, within fifteen minutes! Load the barbell with your maximum weight. This is just the warm up. Afterwards, you will do as many rounds as possible of thirty box jumps, thirty burpees, and a 1,500-meter row for the next thirty minutes. Grab your water and a towel! Starting in ten!"

These are words from my CrossFit coach, and I am addicted.

Two years ago, I made a decision to work toward becoming a stronger, more fit woman, as I am now the only parent my daughters have at the moment. I had let go of physical exercise when my husband became too ill to work out because of his cancer treatments. My body became weak as well, and I lost a lot of weight. We had worked out together as a family at a local recreation center and also done a lot of walking and hiking. Keeping physically fit was extremely important to each of us. I did not think it was fair for me to continue on when Harry could not. After Harry died, I had to let go of the guilt, accept that it was okay to start exercising again, and that he would want that for me.

One thing I realized very quickly through exercising is that trying to lift too much weight than you are prepared to handle can lead to problems. Back squatting too heavy a weight can add undue pressure on your back and knees. I have a personal trainer now who teaches me proper techniques to ensure I perform to my highest expectations, safely. Proper technique helps with the ability to increase weights, which leads to more strength and endurance. Also, the pain I was experiencing in my joints began to diminish. Scripture teaches us the importance of exercising our minds as we do our bodies.

Just as your body cannot stand under too much pressure and heavy weight, carrying the weight and worries of the world on our shoulders without seeking holiness in God's word can wreak havoc our bodies as well. The body has a way of responding to the stress and anxiety we carry around unnecessarily. Internalizing unresolved issues we focus upon without release can force the body to adjust under the weight of carrying them. The body emotionally displays the same pain as lifting too heavy a weight.

When our minds are under stress, we may experience fatigue, shaking, insomnia, heart disease, eating disorders, loneliness, depression, headaches, upset stomachs, forgetfulness, inability to focus, or memory loss. And that's just the tip of the iceberg. I have experienced many of these. I have to remind myself to cast my cares and worries upon the Lord. Remembering to not conform to this world, but to renew my mind (Romans 12:2). The way I practice these disciplines is to trust and seek God's direction and protection through devotions and prayers to Him. Reading His word. I must also practice forgiveness, compassion, and understanding of others and myself.

Allow the Lord to take care of your burdens. Relieve your body of the aches and pains carrying the weight of struggles and hardships upon your shoulders. You will be a healthier, stronger you.

> *Give all your cares to the Lord and He will give you strength. He will never let those who are right with Him be shaken.*

> PSALM 55:22 (NLV)

PICKING UP SCRAPS

*W*hen you see a penny on the ground, do you stop and pick it up? I know for a fact that I have passed over a penny many times. Many pennies can add up to a lot of change, and I do not always pass up change. Instead, I count it. It is better to have one penny than no pennies at all.

After divorce in my family as a young girl, money was hard to come by. Food stamps and taxi cabs to school for a season were stark reminders of a lack of pennies. Still to this day, when I see a penny on the ground, I contemplate whether to pick it up or not. Sometimes I will place one on the ground for a young person to discover. To some it may seem like a scrap, small change, something worthless, but to a poor individual, it can be seen as a treasure.

SCRAPS: *Worthless materials to be disposed of, small piece of something that is left over after the rest has been used.*

A few months ago, I traveled to Uganda to the city of Pader. We were on mission to take clothing to families living in small cell groups of men, women, and children. We purchased food for them with the monies donated by the members of the Austin Ridge Church. On this particular trip there were only two of us who traveled: Holly, the founder of Women of Pader, a nonprofit organization, and myself. Our trip also included a daylong women's conference with translators. Songs were sung, dances were danced, Scripture was read, testimonies were shared, and tears were shed. I fell in love with my new brothers and sisters in Christ.

The women in the community had been taught to make certain pieces to jewelry that in turn would be brought back to the States and sold, so they could earn an income and provide for the needs of their families. Their pieces were beautiful, and they used every bit of material available to them in their designs. Even the leftover scraps.

Another woman caught my attention when walking through the town. A beautiful seamstress and dress maker. She was sewing with a vintage machine and had fabric hanging inside the walls of her shop for choices of color and design. I desperately wanted to have a beautiful dress like the other women in town, so I approached her and chose my design, then she measured me for the fit. Later that day I stopped back in for a visit to see her progress. She was sewing my dress, and I saw the leftover scraps on the ground by her feet. I was so honored and excited to have my dress to bring home to the States. I asked her about the scraps on the ground. Would she have enough to make a head piece out of it for me? She reached down, picked up the cloth, and measured my head, then nodded yes with a huge smile. We both saw the worth in those leftover scraps. I still treasure that dress and head wrap hanging in my closet back at home.

I am so thankful our Lord does not consider us worthless scraps—used and disposable. We are worth more than that to Him. He bends down and picks us up to clear off the dust, dents, and rust from a life that is worn and overlooked. He considers us His prized possessions and collects all of us from all corners of the world, polishes us, and calls us His own. He has many shiny pennies. And combined together, their worth is innumerable. You are indeed a shiny penny treasured by the King!

> *"Look at the birds of the air; they neither sow nor reap nor gather into barns, and yet your heavenly Father feeds them. Are you not of more value than they?"*
>
> MATTHEW 6:26

Red Light, Green Light

*S*ometimes it's hard to know when you are supposed to stop and when you are supposed to go. Just as difficult, can be the waiting period that lingers in between. Taking a step forward while looking back over your shoulder is an indicator of the uncertainty and unsure footing ahead. If only we could see what the near or distant future held! Wouldn't life be much easier? Do you really think so?

What about the little surprises that life brings—all the beautiful experiences we look forward to. If revealed beforehand, they would certainly spoil the occasion. Just like someone giving a secret away when they have sworn not to tell. The excitement of the surprise would be lost. If we could see into the future, we might or might not like what we see. I suppose there is a positive side to not knowing whether we should stop or go. If we didn't like what we saw, we might come to a screeching halt, dig our heels into the dirt and start backpedaling.

I don't know about you, but I am sure I would not like finding out how much time I would have to live or when I would be called home. What if tragedy was a part of the future in our lives or the lives of our loved ones? Really, think about that. If we could not change the circumstances or change the outcome, we probably wouldn't be able to carry on. Helplessness, defeat, sadness, and possibly fear would overwhelm us, and we wouldn't be of help to anyone.

God protects us by making sure our eyes are shielded from being able to see into our future. He asks us to trust Him completely with His plan for our life. That does not mean we should sit still and not do anything. It requires action on our part when He says go. When He says stop, we should stop. Sometimes He asks us to be patient and just wait. Are you just as guilty as I am about running right through a yellow light because of a lack of patience?

The dreaded waiting period is probably the most difficult of all three scenarios. Sometimes God says to wait. There may even be a season of silence. The challenge will be to sit tight and wait for either a green light that says go or a red light that tells us to stop. We can be certain that whether God says stop or go, He has our very best interest at heart.

> *Wait for the Lord; be strong and let your heart take courage; yes, wait for the Lord.*

> PSALM 27:14 (NASB)

LENSES

*L*enses in our eyes capture the beauty of this world in its true vibrant color. More expensive cameras with the very best lens can usually capture an image with the closest imprint as possible, but not as human lenses can. How many times have we heard a picture doesn't do an experience justice? My iPhone 7S has a pretty good lens in it, but it cannot capture the true color. Therefore, I get to practice enhancing, saturating, cropping, and lightening the image to make it as close as possible to what my natural lenses see.

Sunglass lenses transfer even a different view. We wear dark shades to cover our eyes and protect them from the bright sun, but they also cast a hue that alters the way we see everything. I have chosen an almost translucent blue to wear on cloudy days because I simply adore color and capturing the world around me in all of its vibrant beauty. Cheap sunglasses, rose-colored glasses, aviators—sunglasses come in different shades and sizes to enhance and protect our God-given lenses.

For some of us, our lenses are damaged or have fallen to disease. We are color blind, we see through cataracts, or we devastatingly do not see at all. Our learned knowledge, surgery, or memory carries us through our vivid lens. Eye lenses are extremely important, as they are the windows to our soul. Protecting them and servicing them is a priority.

In the Scriptures God shielded, and even caused blindness, in people's eyes when He wanted to demonstrate His glory. He is shielding our eyes this very moment from seeing the supernatural spiritual realm. If He unshielded our eyes, it would probably cause such fear and awe, that we would fall as a dead man just as John did when he saw Jesus in all His glory. Oh, what a day that will be when our eyes will look upon God and Jesus in all their glory in the heavenly places. For now, by faith we know They are there though we can't see Them.

In the day of the Lord, all eyes shall see, every knee will bow, and every tongue will confess the truth and acknowledge the Lord as Savior and Messiah. How do we know? Scripture is very clear about that.

TERRI LYNN SCHMIDT

The great prophets and disciples of the Old and New Testaments tell us time and time again of the men and women whose eyes witnessed the glory of our Lord in person. Oh, if only I could capture a glimpse in our humanly, earthly realm. On that day trumpets will sound, and the sky will be rolled back as a scroll and Christ will return descending in the clouds.

Have you heard of this day? Are you looking through the lenses of your eyes upon that approaching day? On that day our Lord will gaze upon us and look into the windows of our soul through our eyes and directly into our hearts. What will He find? If you do not know the significance of that day, ask God to reveal truth to you and take you through the process of increasing your knowledge and by speaking directly to your heart. By confessing and asking for forgiveness of sin, with believing by faith in the Truth, His Son, you *will* be set free and see this world and all its beauty through a brand-new gift set of lenses! No one can snatch that away from you. God keeps you in the palm of His hand to make certain of that.

> *But as it is written: "Eye has not seen, nor ear heard,*
> *nor have entered into the heart of man the things*
> *which God has prepared for those who love Him."*

1 CORINTHIANS 2:9

A TUNNEL

*T*HERE is light at the end of the tunnel. There IS light at the end of the tunnel There is LIGHT at the end of the tunnel. There is light AT the end of the tunnel. There is light at the END of the tunnel. Finally. Yes, I can see the Light at the end of the TUNNEL. Many songs were written and phrases uttered referring to the process of traveling through a tunnel. References mostly address our levels of hope in times of despair and desperately seeking a light.

Tunnels are dark and your sight is limited. Short distances through a tunnel are most welcoming where long congested paths through a tunnel can cause anxiety. We go through these tunnels together. As a dear friend reminds me quite often, "Breathe, relax, and pray. All will be fine." I am with you on this journey and so is another who keeps His eye on us so much more than on the sparrows. Remember, He will stay with us and will not leave us during this season when we are experiencing darkness.

Tunnels are carved out of mountains and some are built under highways or under airport strips. The purpose of a tunnel carved beneath a structure is to help shorten our travel distance. Can you imagine if today we had to trek over and across miles and heights of mountains to get to the next town? Yes, the larger the mountain, the longer the tunnel. Even still, this time of distance is shorter than if we had to go over or around the obstruction. Tunnels are beautiful and strong. Their structures are substantial.

Driving from sunlight into a dark tunnel, your eyes have to adjust. Headlights on our vehicles automatically come on and lead the way for our safety. The Light of the world provides our guidance and levels of comfort until we approach the end of our dark tunnel. Stories have been told of a Light seen through a tunnel when someone has had a near death experience. Only our Lord knows the duration of our travel time through particular tunnels. Your tunnel may be short and quick whereas mine may go on for several miles. One thing for certain, we travel them together with God's help. Keep your eyes focused on the Light and the darkness will soon come to an end.

TERRI LYNN SCHMIDT

The Light shines in the darkness, yet the darkness did not overcome it.

JOHN 1:5

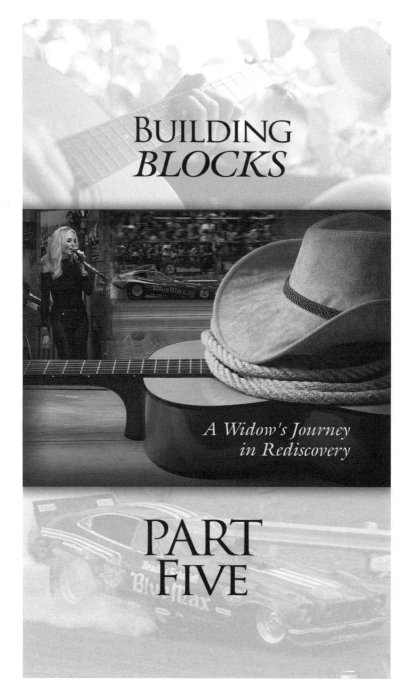

BUILDING
BLOCKS

*A Widow's Journey
in Rediscovery*

PART
FIVE

TERRI LYNN SCHMIDT

COMMITMENT

*T*he word commitment stares us in the face every single day. Basically, our lives are saturated with decisions based upon our willingness to commit. To believe is to commit. To have faith is to commit. To step out of your comfort zone is to commit. Starting a new business, exercise program, marriage, or family takes commitment. Goodness, even putting both feet on the floor to step out of bed takes a committed action. Yet, we run—and run hard—from it!

Making a decision to commit means taking a risk and putting ourselves in a position of either achieving success or accepting failure. Yet, it is within these commitments that blessings flow. Flow in abundance indeed. Without even the tiniest commitment, we can shrivel up and become a useless vessel. We have no idea what is going to take place in the future. But it all boils down to a more grandioso action—a decision.

If it seems I have repeated my most challenging word many times in my writing, you are correct. Making decisions and then following through with commitment has been an ongoing struggle of mine. These shortcomings have affected my life and the lives of those the closest to me. On the outside of my intimate inner circle, I believe others have benefited or suffered based upon my level of commitment. The ripple effect could possibly be enormous, unbeknownst to me.

How do we overcome the fear of commitment? Overcoming the inability to commit comes down to three common words we hear so often, yet they are extremely powerful: Faith. Hope. Love. Mix in a little trust with that recipe and you have a wonderfully balanced outcome. Each action and feeling hangs in the balance of the decision to commit to all. Let's use our Lord and Savior, His Father, and His mother, Mary, as a beautiful example.

Mary was a young Nazarene woman who had not known a man and was betrothed to a carpenter named Joseph. An angel sent by God, Gabriel, appeared to Mary and called her highly favored and blessed among women. He announced that she was chosen by God to carry and give birth to His Son, who would be called Jesus. Mary was faced with a critical decision that would require a solid commitment, one that literally would change the outcome of the world!

Can you imagine what would have happened had she said no and ran in the opposite direction? Instead, Mary decided to submit herself to God's will, the Holy Spirit overshadowed her, and she conceived a child according to what was spoken. Her faith and trust in God pole-vaulted the *entire nation* into a season of hope and love. The story of her commitment to carry God's child for nine months, regardless of her fear of success or failure in the eyes of her witnesses, will forever be told. Let's learn from her dedicated devotion.

> *Then the angel said to them, "Do not be afraid, for behold, I bring you good tidings of great joy which will be to all people. For there is born to you this day in the city of David a Savior, who is Christ the Lord."*

LUKE 2:10–11

THE ROCK

*I*mage yourself in a village, digging a water well to reach the source in order to quench the thirst of all those around you watching and waiting. Suddenly you hit a layer of very thick rock. It will not budge, it will not move. You have tried every tool in your belt to get that rock to loosen. You need that water to burst forth with abundance. You become discouraged, and everyone is waiting to see what you will do, knowing the critical situation at hand. If the people do not get the water they need, they could perish.

What would you do? Retreat? Accept defeat?
Say, I'm sorry, we tried everything?

Turning around, locking eyes with, and studying the faces of those who are desperate and thirsty for water, determination kicks in and you just can't give up. You resume chipping and drilling away at that rock, giving all that you've got with as much force as you can apply. Just then, in that very moment of the final blow, a tiny pinhole is breached and releases a trickle. That little trickle builds up pressure underneath, all around that tiny fracture. As the pressure increases with intensity, an explosion takes place, breaking through all the hard rock that prevented the well from flowing freely.

In a recent experience I personally wasn't trying to dig a well, but the visual I had, helped me in making a dramatic decision that in turn was going to affect a lot of people. When people are counting on you and your actions could either bring forth water or dry up a land, it is extremely important to go to the solid Rock for support and guidance. Make sure you have a solid rock to stand upon when you are faced with really tough decisions. If you have been called to a task or a mission, remain faithful until the Rock gives you a way to abundance.

> *"Though the rain comes in torrents, and the floods rise, and the storm winds beat against this house, it won't collapse, for it is built on rock."*

MATTHEW 7:25 (TLB)

TERRI LYNN SCHMIDT

PERSEVERANCE

"When the going gets tough, the tough get going." I have seen it over and over again. The song "Some Like It Hot" by The Power Station goes, "Some like it hot, and some sweat when the heat is on. Some feel the heat and decide that they can't go on ... Feel the heat pushing you to decide." What do you do when you feel the heat? Ready or not!

Leaders find whatever it takes to persevere and continue to follow hard after their ambition. Perseverance is not always easy to acquire; many times, it must be learned through personal development. It takes inner strength to reach down deep inside your soul and take ownership. Mastering this character trait takes discipline—determining that nothing can cause you to waiver or quit.

It occurred to me one morning after reading through my daily devotion that "desire ... without discipline or knowledge will result in my remaining stagnant with no direction. I cannot move forward without self-discipline." Steadfast perseverance. Oh my!

When you feel the intense pressure needed to persevere, do you cave...or do you buckle down? I am asking you this question for a reason. Being a huge visionary myself, I know what I personally have to do to push toward making my visions become a reality. Far too many people settle for less than what they have envisioned their lives to be.

At times, I have lost faith in my ability to believe and to follow through. I revert back to the teachings, training, and vision that captured me in the beginning for direction. Remarkably though, when push comes to shove and my feet are held to the fire, the survival and boldness needed to press on takes over and I am able to face that fear straight on. Nothing can hold me back. Nothing.

Do you stay and fight—or take flight—when the heat is on? The inner turmoil is raging. Fear that has been created paralyzes us. The question we are all faced with when trying to transfer our visions into reality is, Do I have what it takes to persevere? Ask yourself another question: How bad do I really want it? Remember that fear of man is not from God. That is a lie straight from the Enemy. The only fear God requires of us is an obedient, reverent fear of Him!

It is simply amazing that when we are backed into a corner with nowhere else to turn, we take hold of our vision that is about to escape through the window and pull it back in. We really do want to hold on to it and not let it go! I challenge you to go back and revisit your vision. Do not let it escape out of your reach. Revisit it, rope it back in, and feel the heat, then decide to go on. No matter what it takes, never quit. Persevere!

> *I have fought the good fight, I have finished the race,*
> *I have kept the faith.*

2 TIMOTHY 4:7

STEERING

*F*or the last month I have been taking lessons on boat maneuvering in order to take friends and family out on the lake this summer. Very challenging to say the least! Turning the wheel in the right direction, looking over my shoulder to check the direction the motor is facing, and steering clear of docks and other boats in their slips completely wears on my nerves. Steering a boat is a lot different than steering a car. I now know the importance of having the boat react to my steering to make sure everyone in my boat is safe on the water.

On one of my drives recently, I was heading south on I-35 toward Austin one evening when the flow of traffic came to a sudden halt. As I was approaching the single-file lane, I noticed burned tire skid marks for hundreds of feet on the roadway and chunks of broken concrete from the wall lining the highway. An eighteen-wheeler with six cars stacked and in tow had come to an abrupt stop in the right lane of a winding section. Though I do not know the details, my best guess is that he had taken his eyes or hands off the steering wheel for a few seconds and brushed up against the concrete wall. He possibly could have very easily put many lives in danger with his poor driving.

I wonder if sometimes we take our eyes off the road ahead of us during those critical moments. Moments that can be life changing in one split second. Whenever the road is wide open, straight, and moving at a steady pace, we go into autopilot mode and get careless. Maybe we only have one hand on the wheel. Yet as the road narrows and begins to twist and wind, we grip the steering wheel tighter with both hands, white-knuckled. Our eyes are straightforward. Controlling the steering is our responsibility to everyone around us.

I admit that I have wondered what it would feel like to close my eyes and take my hands off the steering wheel. To just let go. Even though I am most certain I know what the outcome would be, I get so tired of steering the wheel sometimes. And getting into a tug of war with God on the wheel and swerving all over the road is probably not a very good idea. Instead, just like Carrie Underwood sings about in "Jesus Take the Wheel," I want to hand the wheel over to Him and let Him steer me in the direction He wants me to go. Surely the direction He would take me would be far better than the one of my choosing.

Relinquish, concede, and if you have to, move to the passenger seat. With God behind the wheel steering our boats, our cars, our lives, He will steer us to safety.

Holding on to faith and a good conscience, which some have rejected and so have suffered shipwreck with regard to the faith.

1 TIMOTHY 1:19 (NIVUK)

TIME

Hurry up! Slow down!
Don't just sit there, do something!
Don't do anything, just stand there.
I wish I had more time!
I wish that day would come already!

Time marches on, time stands still. When you experience the loss of a loved one or the thrill of a newborn life, have you ever wanted time to stop and not move at all? Have you thought about what would happen if time actually did come to a halt? We would all remain in our current circumstance and not begin to heal, to move past the pain, to plan, experience, laugh, or grow. Time has a way of forcing us to move from where we are. Try as we may, we cannot force time to remain on our side or place it in a bottle and put it on a shelf.

Depending on what is happing in your life right now, time is either at an excruciating crawling pace or time is running full speed ahead, adding along with it a level of stress. We all find ourselves somewhere at the beginning or at the end of one of those spectrums. Maybe you are right in the middle of that pendulum swing. Let's spend some *time* in this space.

Tim McGraw's song "Live Like You Were Dying" begs the question, what did you do with *it*? Time, that is. We learn through the lyrics that the person who has just been given the news that his life is coming to an end evaluates the time he has left and decides that he is going to make the most of it. He does all the activities he always wanted to do. He reconciles broken relationships and becomes the person he wanted to be by making the necessary changes needed to do just that.

Where do you spend most of your time? Are you wasting away precious minutes, or are you utilizing this gift wisely? Someone needs a kind word from you. Others need a cup of cold water. Many need the abundance of clothing you have hanging in your closet. Bare feet could be covered with those old shoes you have no use for anymore. Someone with a broken heart needs your smile and hug. We can't stop the hands of time, but we can decide today how we are going to use it. Time is a gift that has been entrusted to us. What are you going to do with it? Make the most of it!

> *See then that you walk circumspectly, not as fools*
> *but as wise, redeeming the time, because the days are*
> *evil. Therefore, do not be unwise, but understand*
> *what the will of the Lord is.*
>
> EPHESIANS 5:15–17

COLLABORATION

COLLABORATION:
*Working with each other to do a task
and to achieve shared goals.
To work jointly with others or together
especially in an intellectual endeavor.*

After attending the Formula One races in Austin, Texas, I was sitting outside in a round setting talking about different cultures in the racing worlds with new friends from Mexico and Spain when our conversation landed on the word *collaboration*. The discussion was based upon all people from across the world coming together with one common interest. One thing I have learned by spending time with professional racers, whether it be NHRA or NASCAR or learning about the Formula One mind-set, they have one common denominator: team effort and extreme mechanical engineering intelligence. They understand the concept of working together to achieve elaborate goals. The drivers can only go as fast as the car and the crew behind the mechanics of the car.

The world teaches that being independent and working solo is a sign of strength and courage. You don't need anyone to take care of you. You can do it yourself, all by yourself. You can't trust anyone, and if you want a job done right, you have to just get out there and get it done. How many times have we all heard these words during our years of growing into maturity? The truth is that this is far from the truth. Going solo is a very lonely place to be. We were never intended to be a solo act and tread through this life alone. We were made to work as a community in collaboration with each other for a greater purpose.

I have discovered that asking for help is not a sign of weakness. In fact, not asking for help is a sign of pride. It demonstrates that I think I can handle everything on my own. In these days and times of setting goals and planning a strategy, it is definitely a good idea to ask for help. Pressing forward with a greater purpose in mind takes a village of people to set the thoughts and ideas into motion. It takes a whole team effort. I am thankful I have come to realize the importance of collaboration.

TERRI LYNN SCHMIDT

If you are a person working in a position where month end numbers are critical to your income and job position, then you understand the importance of working closely with others. Going at it alone would not be a very good idea during that time. Christ understood the importance of joint efforts when He sent His disciples out at least two at a time. The apostle Paul always had like-minded companions on his journeys into hostile countries. Remember, the next time you need to reach out and ask for help in accomplishing a goal, task, or mission, you will be demonstrating strength, not weakness.

> *Two are better than one, because they have a good reward for their labor. For if they fall, one will lift up his companion.*

> ECCLESIASTES 4:9–10

PRESSURE

*O*h, the joys of being under pressure. It comes at us from all angles. There are times we feel it from just a few sides, and other times it is pressing in on all sides. Moments like these make us feel like players in a game of dodge ball. It seems everything happens at the same time. If we are not dodging a ball, we definitely are juggling a few.

I have been experiencing a lot of dodging and juggling lately. I wonder sometimes if I do not thrive on the pressures of taking on more than I should. In a sense it makes me feel more alive, having more of a purpose. The simple life of letting each day roll by without one decisive act of accomplishment or activity is just not appealing to me. Can you relate to what I am saying?

A good analogy of the feeling of this type of pressure would be an example of a balloon. When you add pressure to all sides, you can see and feel the tension expanding to near bursting. I definitely know that feeling in my chest when the pressure is on. A little anxiety can become overwhelming. Sometimes when our tension is simply too much to take, we retreat and shut down. We are looking out at the big picture instead of focusing on what is right in front of us at the moment. We forget to take one day at a time.

How are you handling the pressures in your life? Your life just may depend upon it. I know a few young people in their early twenties who are having anxiety attacks because of pressure and tension, and they see their futures as uncertain. It concerns me to know that they are so fearful and so full of worry that their bodies are reacting and shutting down. To them it feels as if they are having heart attacks. They are on medication to help them relax and not have total meltdowns. That is alarming to me.

When it comes to handling pressure, I get alone. I have my quiet time, reading promises of Scripture. I sit still and listen to the songs of the birds and remember that God takes care of them and He is very aware of my needs and concerns. I remember we all have a purpose, and everything happens for a reason to expand and grow us into what we are supposed to become. I remind myself that God is still in control, and my life is in His grip. I take one day at a time and stay focused on the matters at hand instead of the overwhelming big picture. I take a deep breath, sigh, and then smile because I choose courage and boldness, and put one foot in front of the other each day. Then, I jump back in!

I pray the same for you.

"Therefore, do not worry about tomorrow, for tomor- row will worry about its own things. Sufficient for the day is its own trouble."

MATTHEW 6:34

DEADLINES

DEADLINE:
*The latest time or date by which
something should be completed.
Making sure before the day is over
what needs to be done.*

The world would be total chaos without deadlines. We would put off a project dear to our hearts, give up on achieving that goal we desire, and—heaven forbid—stay in bed all day without a responsibility or care in the world to anybody or anything. We could choose to just not show up, but deadlines nudge us out of our comfort zones. Without them we would remain stagnant and cease to strive for higher expectations.

My daughters are both heading off to college this year, one to The University of Alabama and the other to Arizona State University. There is a certain time frame in which tuition has to be paid, parking passes have to be purchased, and housing has to be moved in to. As for me, there is a certain time to cry, and then there is a day to pick my heaving body up off the floor, dry the tears, and get going. Without a deadline for college entrance, I could hold my daughters hostage and refuse to let them out of my sight. This would obviously keep them from growing and becoming the young women God intended them to be. We all have deadlines. Thank goodness!

You may have the type of personality that strives to accomplish a task way before the set time of completion. You make it your priority to get it done so far in advance that it becomes the least of your worries. You have figured it out. Life without stress has freed you to accomplish more than you could have ever expected. You are blissfully happy and full of joy. You are way ahead of the game. You are what I desire to be.

Or maybe you are a someone who procrastinates. You push the limit to the thirteenth hour and come sliding in to home base feet first. Sounds like someone I know really well. *Smile.* Is the responsibility too much to bear? Are you fearful that project you propose will be a huge success? Are you afraid that you just might reach that goal you set out to accomplish? If you believe that you were created for this moment in time for this purpose, do it anyway. Feel the fear and then do it anyway.

I don't know about you, but I am thankful for deadlines. They force me to start moving and keep going. They force me to decide when I had rather crawl into a hole. They encourage me to choose between life or actually living. The next time a deadline approaches, look it straight in the eye and say, "I welcome you, embrace you, laugh at you, tackle you, wrestle with you, and respect you. You make me reach, climb, achieve, stretch, and grow."

> *"For My thoughts are not your thoughts, nor are your ways My ways," says the Lord. "For as the heavens are higher than the earth, so are My ways higher than your ways, And My thoughts higher than your thoughts."*
>
> ISAIAH 55:8–9

STAND UP, SPEAK UP, GROW UP!

*N*egativity can be representative of jealously, envy, self-pity, anger, bitterness, or playing the victim role. A lot of these characteristics are running rampant in our society today. One finger pointing forward at an accuser always has four pointing directly back. Positive? Negative? Where do you reside? In contrast, positivity is a mind-set whereby you focus only on the positive circumstances in your life. Perfection is not possible on this side of heaven; however, you can train your mind to search for the good in others and your surroundings. In doing so, empathy and compassion take precedence over dwelling on imperfections. The grace we have received at the cross is the grace we extend toward others.

My television remains in the off mode—all the time—to divert my thinking toward only the good in this world. Making that claim may lead someone to think I am naïve and pretty clueless in keeping up with the current times. I started thinking about this a few days ago. Hmmm. I decided that I had a responsibility to my fellow man and country to be in the know and that my claim was probably not the smartest choice of words as a responsible adult. Could someone actually have an intelligent conversation with me on these matters? Having relied on reading other people's views to draw my opinions, it was time that I stood up so that I could speak up! So ... I grew up and turned my TV on. Shocking, I know!

Earlier in this book, I featured my daughters expressing their idea of hope. In a similar way, I have asked three of the following individuals, whose viewpoints on these topics I have read in their written expressions, to share their thoughts on the matter. I respectfully refer to them as "Positive, Realistic, and Prayer Warrior."

Dave Jacobs: *It's easy to focus on the good, but never forget the fallen. The world is what you make of it. If it doesn't fit, make alterations. These uncertain times can test the level of anxiety in anyone, but to me and my LLC organization, The*

TERRI LYNN SCHMIDT

Positive Side, it's a matter of pursuing happiness for all those who did not come home.

Steve Dutton: *Destruction of conservatism has driven our country to the edge of the abyss. A blind eye, pacifism, and a quiet demeanor toward an election will likely find our country and us at the bottom of such with no hope or ability to climb out. Our influence of principles and values, derived from our beliefs, can influence the direction of our country.*

Linda Churchwell: *Ah, balance. It's the mature place whole-seekers strive toward, and where our example in total perfection, Jesus Christ, constantly resides. The Christian's goal is to be like Him, and influence our world, right? Extremism in any direction detracts us from the goal; positivity becomes insensitivity to other's suffering, while negativity deceives. Seasons of unmitigated joy and peace, as well as seasons of pain, pepper the true Christians life—and we "GROW UP." We're told to "rejoice with those who rejoice, and weep with those who weep" in Romans 12:15. Balance brings peace out of chaos, and His love to a dying world.*

"Stand up, speak up, grow up."

Putting those three phrases together gave me a new sense of determination. I need to be held accountable in seeking out ways of equipping myself with information needed to help find a solution, thus instilling more positivity into a fallen world of violence, hatred, and chaos. God is *still* on the throne. He is watching over us and sees everything. And one day, we will be accountable to Him for our actions and words or the lack thereof.

These things I have spoken unto you, that in me ye might have peace. In the world ye shall have tribulation: but be of good cheer; I have overcome the world.

JOHN 16:33 (KJV)

80/20 RULE

*M*y closet at home is at more than 100 percent capacity, and I only wear maybe 20 percent of the clothing and shoes I have accumulated throughout the years. I use only about 20 percent of the living space in my home: my bedroom, kitchen, utility room, and garage. About 20 percent of your team members or employees will do 80 of the work for your business, and 20 percent of church members will carry the weight of the entire congregation with teaching, programs, financial support, missions, and tithes. Goodness! What about that remaining 80 percent? Do we just kick the 80 percent to the curb? Stuff, yes. People, no.

Let's come at this from a different angle. The 80/20 rule can also apply to relationships. I definitely am not an expert, nor do I have a degree in psychology, but I do study body language and can peer deep into the soul of another to see their fears, hurts, and just about every other emotion. Maybe because I see in others what I can see in myself. We all desire to be loved, approved, and needed; we want to feel important and receive affirmation that we matter. We do have a purpose. We are designed to be relational. Looking through spiritual eyes, we can find the good in all people.

I believe in my heart that we have the capacity to love more than one person in our lifetime. Choosing to love only *one* person in a covenant marriage before God is a lifetime commitment: "till death do you part." Choosing that person to move into a covenant with is a serious matter. I didn't intend to apply the 80/20 rule in my mind-set toward relationships until after I became a widow. Entering the single life and dating world again after twenty years of marriage was an eye-opener. Terms like *love of my life*, *the one*, and *soul mate* were tossed to and fro and were so commonly used in a nonchalant manner. Here is my personal approach in determining a Mr. Right.

Faith in the Lord is nonnegotiable. Adventure is important. Honesty is important. Trust is important. Faithfulness is important. Integrity is important. Compatibility is important. Laughter is important, especially at yourself. Vision is important. Being on the same path is important.

Friendship is important, and chemistry is the natural progression when all these attributes are in place. I consider these "musts" to be the 80 percent. The remaining 20 percent needs to be broken down into 10 and 10. The first 10 percent is where compromise steps in. Where are you going to live? Who will have which responsibility? Who is going to bend and allow the other person their will and desire? TV time? Entertainment time? You know, putting the other person's needs before your own. At this point, the 80 has now become 90 percent. You are heading in the right direction. What we have left to determine is the remaining 10 percent. I see this as the no-go zone.

If you find yourself having to compromise your integrity, compromise your morals, question facts that surface which do not line up with truth, things are not aligning with Scripture, and there are no indications of change prompting a move into the right direction ... stop. It is time to reevaluate and determine whether the remaining 10 percent has just deemed the 90 percent null and void. This process is not easy, but the sooner you come to your conclusion the more pain you will be able to spare the both of you.

As I stated earlier, I am not a certified life coach, but I do hope that something resonates with you in a helpful way. Certainly, there is a life coach who has both people's interests at heart, and that is our heavenly Father, whose guidebook is the Bible. He knows all and wants to help save us from unnecessary pain as well. Ask Him to help guide you through the 80/20 rule on relationships. He already has an answer. Go or stop.

> *Finally brethren, whatever things are true, whatever things are noble, whatever things are just, whatever things are pure, whatever things are lovely, whatever things are of good report, if there is any virtue and if there is anything praiseworthy, meditate on these things.*

> PHILIPPIANS 4:8–9

HUMILITY

"*You* are not the boss of me." "I am going to show you who's in charge if it's the last thing I do!"

Comments of a heart determined to remain in control no matter what. We like to think we are in complete control of our lives. We have control over our jobs, control over our finances, control over family, the weather, stock market, housing programs, world hunger, gas prices and so on. Do you see how quickly we can spiral out of control? What about when "life" happens ...unexpectedly? The loss of a house, health, or life? Then what?

The things we can control are our words, our attitudes, our spending habits, and the way we treat the people in our lives. Especially the ones closest to us. What if you were faced with the decision of someone's advancement over your own personal gain? Are you willing to sit on the back row and be a cheerleader for the greater good of the team in your entire organization? Sometimes we must sit in the back seat and let someone else take the steering wheel.

My husband is an inductee of the National Hot Rod Association hall of fame. As the owner and chief mechanic of the Blue Max funny car, he did not physically drive the car. He gave control over to the driver who physically had to set the car in motion. Though Harry was the owner and had the vision of launching the car into its infamous reputation, he had to choose to take the backseat and stand off in a distance out of the way to let the driver have the spotlight. He was the cheerleader with his communication and support for the driver who led his team to success.

Suppose the driver of a race car thought he wanted to prove to his team that he was the one completely in control of the win and did not need any help. He could choose to sit on the starting line determined not to move when the green light appears. His move could paralyze the implementation and the entire team. Refusal to accept instruction or guidance on flipping the switch even robs the car of what it was built to do. The driver must decide to lay his pride aside, humble himself under instruction, flip that switch and push full speed ahead to the finish line for the greater good of the whole race team. Shifting through the gears, the tires start burning and the engine accelerates to maximum RPMs. Pulling the parachute as he crosses the finish line, he receives a cheer from the crowd and from his team.

Who is steering your vehicle? Have you humbled yourself and slipped into the backseat for the best Driver to take control? With God behind the wheel you are sure to cross the finish line as a winner.

> *But he who is greatest among you shall be your ser-*
> *vant. And whoever exhalts himself will be humbled,*
> *and he who humbles himself will be exhalted.*

MATTHEW 23:11-12

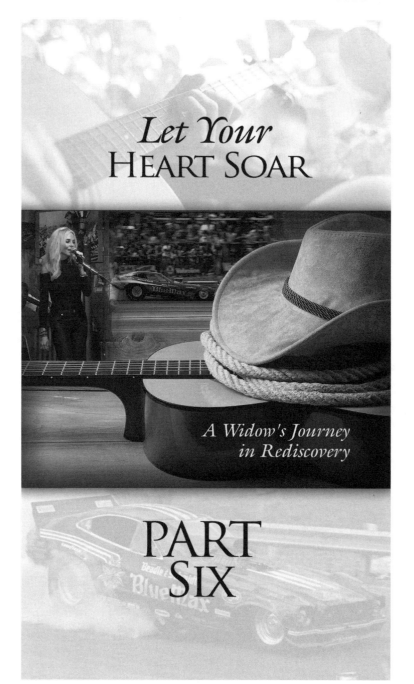

Let Your
HEART SOAR

*A Widow's Journey
in Rediscovery*

PART
SIX

TERRI LYNN SCHMIDT

SPARKLE
AND SHINE

*T*he sparkle in your eye is like the sparkle of a beautiful diamond. The human eye is naturally drawn to things that sparkle. Whether it be a person or an item. We just can't help it.

I received two different birthday cards last month from two separate friends with the endearment on the front cover being all about the word *sparkle*. I even apply a sparkle glitter lotion to my arms before heading out the door for an event because I like to shine. Right this very moment I have sparkles in my nail polish. Guess I am obsessed as well!

What makes you sparkle and shine? (And yes, men shine as well.) If you are full of life, animated, bubbly, and witty, then I suppose you are radiantly beaming with that sparkle that gets everyone looking your way. It's ok to smile if this perfectly describes you. You are helping to spread the message of fun-loving happiness. In today's world we can all certainly use a large of dose of that joy you project.

Have you ever had to dig deep down into dirt and pull out that rough diamond to have it polished for a sparkle? Oh boy, I know I certainly have. Being rough around the edges for a certain amount of time is not any fun at all. We project what we perceive to be reality. Our shine can get a little dimmed when we get overwhelmed. Sometimes we have to put forth every ounce of energy in our effort to shine. Especially when you just do not feel like it.

Some people have a certain shine about them that is evident of the Light taking up residence inside. They can't help but burst forth with a sparkle no one can diminish. We are drawn to them and want to be around them. The Light from their shine brings warmth and comfort. The laughter of a Sparkler or Sparklerette is very contagious, and before you know it, you are laughing right along with them. You may need to surround yourself with these amazing shining stars to help you rekindle yours. Lay down your overwhelmed soul and let the Light reflect upon you until your diamond is no longer rough, but polished to shimmer and shine!

"Let your light so shine before men, that they may see your good works and glorify your Father in heaven."

MATTHEW 5:16

SILHOUETTES

*H*ues of vibrant red and deep blue mix with words written in bold white. The sounds and players of violin, guitar, keyboard, and angelic voices are all outlined against the illuminated screen. Silhouettes are evidence of the humble hearts leading the worship time of the service. These silhouettes are not drawing attention to themselves. They are drawing our attention to the main Person who stands in the spotlight. The Holy Spirit hovers. Silhouettes worship.

Sunglasses on, sitting facing the setting sun, my eyes are fixed on silhouettes of couples and singles dining on the outdoor patio. Faces are not recognizable as I watch them move about. Glasses are toasting, and hands are being held. The sunset outlining each figure is bright with rays extending all around its subject. The silhouettes are the focus this time. They are the stars in this ambience. Love is in the air. Silhouettes of love.

Jumping, running, walking, sitting, or standing, our shadow is our personal silhouette. They mimic everything we do and are always nearby. Some are round, and some are tiny. Others are short; still others are very tall. Where there is light, we cannot escape them even if we sit on them! Sometimes they are silly and sometimes they are sad. Still they remain. Embrace your own silhouette because it is always with you. Silhouettes *can be* annoying!

Every person's silhouette takes on a different personality when they know they are being watched, whether they are on a big screen or being viewed under a microscope. Humble or a show-off. They are black and the outline of the object it represents. I can't help but smile as I write. I wish I could show you all the motion pictures that run through my mind at this moment. I have a *huge* imagination! It has been difficult to figure out how to share on this topic with all the different movie scenes in my mind. Reality and responsibility escape me at times with my daydreaming. I should have been a cartoon illustrator!

What does your silhouette reveal about you? If you are standing outside, look at your shadow. Talk to it and ask it questions: Who are you?

TERRI LYNN SCHMIDT

Are you living life to its fullest? Are you choosing happiness? What is your plan of action to make it all happen? What adjustments are you willing to make to stand firm and walk in truth? Of course your shadow will be waiting for *you* to tell it what *you* want it to do. I will be having a little heart-to-heart talk with mine today.

Life on this earth is so precious and short. The sun is shining, birds are chirping, music is playing, flowers are blooming, rivers are flowing, trees are swaying, dogs are barking, coffee is brewing, saints are praying, boats are cruising, balloons are flying, candles are flickering, glasses are being raised, celebrations are beginning. You are living out a motion picture and you are writing the script (with a lot of help from the Big Man upstairs). Let your silhouette dance and take pictures along the way!

When the Lord turned again the captivity of Zion,
we were like them that dream. Then was our mouth
filled with laughter, and our tongue with singing:
then said they among the heathen, The Lord hath
done great things for them.

PSALM 126:1–2 (KJV)

MUSIC

*M*usic runs through my entire being. The instruments, the rhythm, the tempo, the blending—and the lyrics—move me more than anything else. Period. There is so much time and effort put into creating a piece of music. Country just happens to be my favorite at the moment. Lyrics and legends have changed over the years, but the way music moves me into each level of emotion goes without saying a word. In fact, I have been so moved by music today that I have made a complete about-face from the topic I had planned on writing about and I have chosen music.

Music can dictate and change moods quicker than you can change the channel of the station. Whether you like to listen to country, contemporary Christian, old-time rock and roll, or soft rock, each genre creates the emotion it is designed to. Music can move us from tears of sorrow to tears of joy. Tears from newly found love and tears from love distant and lost. When I listen to music, I hear every single instrument and every vocal part that makes up the composition. After many experiences in the recording studio, I also have the visual of how recording takes place. Layering upon layering and stacking upon stacking to make a beautiful rich sound is art in itself. Each piece is extremely important and necessary to complete the whole sound.

How does music move you? Did you know that God Himself instructed the musicians in the Old Testament? He gave instruction on the design and how music was to be played and where. Yes, music has been around for a very long time. We are still reaping blessings that have come to fruition from years and years of progress in the design and production of beautiful musical pieces. Musical selections that have made history take us back as we revisit our memories according to which song was predominant in our lives at that moment in time. I personally remember exactly where I was and who I was with when I hear certain songs.

Last February my dad passed away from cancer and the side effects of living a hard life. Music was his passion, and he passed it down genetically to me. I was blessed to inherit his favorite guitar. As I write,

TERRI LYNN SCHMIDT

I have just placed it back in its holding stand after strumming the strings and thinking of all the beauty he created with this instrument that produced such lovely sounds. I am inundated with thoughts of all the times he held this guitar and put it to use writing and orchestrating songs that were very dear and personal to his heart. I aquired his songs as well. My dad performed at many venues as the opening act. His memory and music live on through me.

Turn off the television, turn up the music, grab hold of that special someone, and dance off into the sunset. Music is a beautiful thing.

His brother's name was Jubal. He was the father of all those who play the harp and flute.

GENESIS 4:21

DANCING

San José, Mexico was beautiful at sunset. Exotic birds soared and waves crashed as I relaxed in the sun with my favorite songs playing on my iPod. Then something caught my eye. Two bougainvillea leaves were swirling around each other as a tiny tornado tossed them around. As the wind increased, the leaves twirled faster; as it decreased, they slowed to a still. As the wind began again, the leaves were drawn closer together and they spun at a faster pace. They were dancing. Pure beauty in the tiniest form.

When was the last time you danced? Have your struggles in life taken the wind right out from underneath your beautiful wings? You have had a hard time hearing the music that strikes up the dance inside you. You no longer twirl, spin, float, or glide to the rhythm of magnificent sounds of instruments—the universal language that we all hear. Ask yourself now, Can I hear the music?

Maybe you don't believe in dancing. If you are like me though, you can see dance in all forms of life. Every piece of creation has rhythm. When a tree is swaying, it has rhythm. Wheat in a field dances to the rhythm of the wind. Some birds perform a dance as the mating season approaches in order to catch the watchful eye of another bird. We are and should be in control of the gesture of dancing that we do. I am speaking right now on the type of dancing that makes your heart soar. Ask yourself again, Can I hear the music? If you are not hearing the music, then ask yourself, "Why am I not hearing?"

Just as God instructed Moses on how to build the tabernacle, He instructed the musicians on how to build their instruments. God Himself created music. The musicians created the dances that followed suit. Dances before the Lord. You, too, can learn to hear the music again and dance like you once did. Whatever has happened in your life that has caused the music to stop, you can let go of it, choose to heal, and find the dance again. If I can do it, I promise you can too. Start by tapping your toe, then put one foot in front of the other and go for it! One step at a time. Dancing is a beautiful thing.

TERRI LYNN SCHMIDT

Then Miriam the prophetess, the sister of Aaron, took the timbrel in her hand; and all the women went out after her with timbrels and with dances.

EXODUS 15:20 (EMPHASIS MINE)

WINGS

*I*t's a bird, it's a plane ... no wait, it's Terri Lynn. Look at me! I am flying! Soaring over my home, the city, reaching higher and higher. Using my arms, I am able to climb high enough toward the heavens. Pausing and hovering as I feel the wind press under me to keep me afloat, I can see all the scurrying that is taking place down below. Please don't wake me. Let me keep my wings just a little longer.

Outside of our dreams, we desire to experience the phenomenon of flight. Skydiving, parasailing, and soaring off of a cliff were designed to offer those adrenaline rushes. Last year my choice was skydiving in Florida. At first fall I heard the instant sounds of rushing wind, then the silence of pure visual beauty followed until touchdown. Of course, pulling the string that triggered the ejection of the parachute was more than welcomed! The parachute provided the wings we needed to soar safely over the landscape and down below for a secure landing. Would I do it again? You betcha!

Orville and Wilbur Wright attempted their first manned aerial flight with an engine they had built on their own in 1903. Their fascination with the studies of a glider pilot launched their study on the theories of flying. The Wright Brothers changed the course of history and made way for mankind to experience flight that once only eagles and all birds of the air were able to enjoy. Thanks to technology, we now have small GoPro cameras that attach to helmets for showcasing a bird's eye view from up above. For the individual fearful of their feet leaving the ground, this allows them the opportunity of experience.

Naturally and beautifully designed wings get my attention. One reason why I chose this particular location for my home is the view outside my large back window. Hawks, along with other birds, glide to and fro above the treetops and below near the water of the cove be-low, blessing my soul and calming my spirit. God Himself designed the strong, powerful, and mighty wings of eagles, cherubim, and seraphim. Many times, the Bible uses descriptive words referring to wings to prioritize our mind-sets toward strength, protection, and sovereignty. All to the glory of God. Man's designed wings are only an imitation of those designed by God. We still maintain a level of respect to those adorned with the natural gift from heaven above.

God Himself refers to His wings as a symbol of His covering in hiding us away for our benefit. Psalm 91:4 tells us, "He shall cover you with His feathers, and under His *wings* you shall take refuge; His truth shall be your shield and buckler" (emphasis mine). This Scripture is always my first thought and prayer when a family member or friend is experiencing hardships or the death of a loved one. I pray this Scripture for you today as well:

> *But they that wait upon the Lord shall renew their*
> *strength; they shall mount up with wings like eagle;*
> *they shall run, and not be weary; they shall walk,*
> *and not faint.*

ISAIAH 40:31 (KJV)

IN DREAMS

*H*ey, wake up! Were you just day dreaming? *The day dreamer:* One who pauses and sets his eyes in a stare out of a window, during daytime hours and has a vision of where he would like to be, *instead* of where he is right now. *The night dreamer:* One who dreams at night and in that dream is capable of doing anything that she considers to be impossible while being awake.

As a young girl, I day dreamed about my prince charming and a fairy-tale wedding in a chapel complete with a ball gown and white gloves. My prince was going to take me from my existing reality to a place far, far away. We would live happily forever. My nighttime dreams consisted of performing on a huge stage with a large audience. I knew every word to every Elvis song, and for that reason I would be chosen to go onstage to perform with him. I have a feeling that I am not the only one who has once had that dream.

You probably remember the moment in time when your carefree laughter and dreams, which were larger than life, were transformed and the reality of life-changing decisions took you on a different path. *If you could*, would you go back and revisit your amazing dreams? Would the picture be painted with different tones and color hues now at this stage in your life? A dream mostly stems from a passion that has taken root in your heart. Think back to the moment you stopped dreaming. Dreaming is not just for the youngsters; it is for all of us.

Right here, right now.

Some people act upon and follow that dream until it develops into a reality. They are living life at full capacity with joy and enthusiasm. We have all heard people say, "Wow! I must be dreaming. This is too good to be true!" For some people, if the dream becomes a reality, the very thought of it coming to fruition scares them. Along with the success of a dream comes the responsibility for that success.

These responsibilities may require change—in lifestyle, position, or possibly location. It may also require a change in character. We have all been through every kind of change you can think of along this path. No one said it would be easy. Turning your dreams into a reality takes work and dedication. Choose today to begin living out your dreams. When you think you are dreaming, but your eyes are wide open, your dreams have become a reality!

> *And so it was, when Gideon heard the telling of the dream and its interpretation, that he worshiped.*

> JUDGES 7:15

FREE

*F*reebird, *free*dom, *free*-spirited, born to be *free*, *free* weights, *free* range, Land of the *Free*, *free*dom of speech, buy one get one *free*, *free* falling, *free* at last! In order to get one *free*, you must purchase another at the full price. "If you'll buy that, I'll throw the Golden Gate in *free*." Thanks for the last one, King George!

Our freedom in America costs this country a massive price at the expense of lost lives. Ultimate freedom from a disease costs us a devastating price: death of our life on this earth. Freedom from damaging relationships can come with a hurtful price. Whatever we are wanting and needing, "freedom from" takes sacrifice, desire, persistence, and prayer. Freedom comes with a price. A lofty price.

What areas of your life do you desire to be set free from? For me, it is freedom from the bondage of certain sins—painful actions and thoughts that cause harm to myself and to others. I also desire to be set free from guilt and regret. "Search me, O God, and know my heart; try me, and know my anxieties; and see if there is any wicked way in me, and lead me in the way of everlasting" (Psalm 139:23–24). That is my continual prayer spoken out loud. Most of the time, we have our own motives, but God sees the motive of the heart. If you are like me, you can instantly tell the moment a word leaves your mouth if it is harmful or helpful to the hearer. I desire freedom. What do you need to be set free from?

In the Old Testament, through Moses' leading, God set the Israelites free. They were set free from the bondage of slavery. In the New Testament, the disciples and captives were set free from imprisonment. After receiving healing, lepers were set free from their disease and were then free to enter back into their villages to be with their families with the freedom to love. My cousin was set free from prison after serving the time required by penalty. Many prayers were answered and tears shed until that day. Sheer rejoicing came afterward. A forgiven saint learns to rejoice in the "freedom" of others, not judgment in the "conviction." We all have bondages we need to set free.

TERRI LYNN SCHMIDT

There is One who left the freedom and comforts of His heavenly home in order to set us free from our bondage. Freedom that was bought with an excruciatingly painful price. Redemption from the bondage of sin cost our Redeemer His life. An exchange took place on that Roman cross. Jesus took the full weight of our bondage of sin upon His spotless, blameless, sinless body so that we could be free. Free from the slavery of our brokenness. Free from the death penalty as those taken captive. The Gospel is free to those who believe. Thank you, my Redeemer, for setting this captive free.

> *"Then you will know the truth, and the truth will set you free."*

JOHN 8:32 (NIV)

GOING HOME

*S*ettled in and resting peacefully this early morning, my grown children have come home for the weekend. Squeaky toys and hyper jumping have come home as well. Homer, my grand pup, brings this fifty-two-year-old woman so much joy and laughter. Grandchildren will come soon enough, as my oldest daughter is receiving her surprise proposal this weekend, so my grand pup will suffice for now. Though my children are adults, having them together under my roof blesses my heart tremendously. Groceries are spilling out of the refrigerator and I love it! As they sleep, I remember what going home meant to me.

A few years ago, I ventured down memory lane by going to visit my childhood homes. I sat in front of each one and reminisced about the past, with its ups and downs, highs and lows, good times and bad. Even as I write, my emotions are in turmoil as to what I should put into print. I struggle with the thoughts between happy and sad. As I share, I will remind myself that we have all gone through difficult times that we would rather let go of and forget. Much less want to talk about. It's true we block out certain memories and stuff pain into our souls. As I express my feelings on my experience of going back home, I apologize ahead of time to precious family members who are about to read into my heart. Please remember these are my perception of memories alone.

Driving down the road leading up to the first home on memory lane in Arcadia Park, I calculated the long distance I walked to and from elementary school. This home is where I learned to ride my bike and played by jumping in the mud puddles next to our yard. Grass clippings made up our make-believe home rooms off the sidewalk. Doodle bugs were fun to play with alongside our family pets: ducks, a goat, gerbils, parakeets, and cats. Our neighborhood was peaceful until the day our family German Shepherd was shot and killed in our backyard. Our whole family was spooked at every outside sound after that incident, and my daddy decided to move us to Grand Prairie.

Grand Prairie. Most of my memories came from this house. We were not allowed to talk at the dinner table. Laughing out loud would land us a "Go stand in the corner" of the wall with nose pointed in. Whippings came from a switch off the tree that we had to go pick out. If we chose too small, Daddy would go and fetch a replacement.

TERRI LYNN SCHMIDT

Our washing machine would walk the floor if we did not sit on top of it during the spin cycle. We did not wear brand-name clothing and weren't even aware of that until it was brought to our attention by our classmates as we matured. When I made the eighth grade cheer squad, it was rumored to be a mistake, and a few of the other cheerleaders tried to help me by enhancing my hairstyle and makeup to make me "fit in." I then became embarrassed of my family home and made all my friends drop me off at the end of the street so I would walk to my house after they were no longer in sight. Still all seemed normal ... until the two-headed monster of alcoholism and unfaithfulness reared its awful head and divorce was the result. My mother, sisters, and I had to use food stamps until Mother could get a job.

Why am I sharing all of this now? I recently visited my beloved extended Vaughn family in Abilene. As we sat in the kitchen and talked through questions I had as a child, they answered and shed more light on details that helped make sense of my memories. Our Abilene family made up almost all of my most loving memories I have from my childhood. Camping, water skiing, fishing, and frog gigging are just a few. As I sat in a side room of their home during my stay, something occurred to me. Good memories, along with the bad, have made me who I am today. As a young adult, I moved away from home to pursue a music career. That move changed the course of my life. I now live in an incredibly beautiful space, and I am grateful. Sometimes I draw strength from my memories as they remind me of what I have overcome. When we are children, we cannot choose our circumstances and environment, but as adults, we have the option to choose.

As a Christian I look forward to "going home" to heaven. Our earthly homes are only temporary dwelling places. My daddy now is my Father in heaven. He awaits all of us and will welcome us into His loving arms. Whatever your current circumstances are or however painful your memories are, we will be able to talk face-to-face with our loving Father and ask all our "why" questions. You can overcome painful memories and choose to learn from them. I am living proof.

"In My Father's house are many mansions; if it were not so, I would have told you. I go to prepare a place for you."

JOHN 14:2

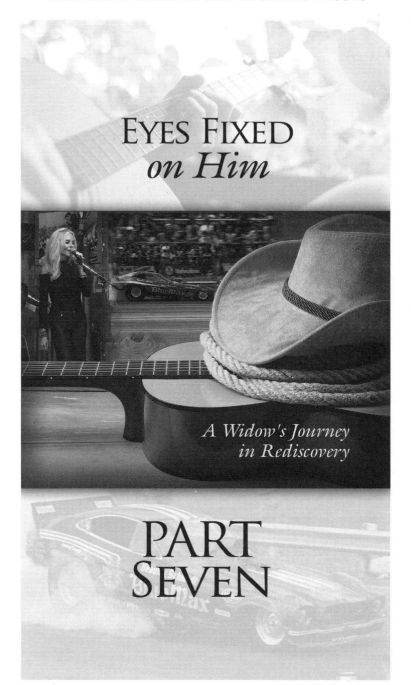

EYES FIXED
on Him

*A Widow's Journey
in Rediscovery*

PART
SEVEN

TERRI LYNN SCHMIDT

HANDS AND FEET

*O*n the aftermath of Hurricane Harvey, our team headed south in Texas to help with recovery and cleanup. Tears filled my eyes as I began preparing for what we would see. After turning my lights off the night before, a thought occurred to me as I laid my head on my pillow. Teams from all over the surrounding areas were already on the scene, along with some firefighter friends, helping remove debris and saturated personal belongings for families who lost almost everything or did lose *everything* that belonged to them. My thoughts were then directed to what I would share from God's Word.

Praying early in the morning several days before, I had thanked God for the hands and feet that I have. Though pain is starting to set in my joints in several places, I will continue to move and go where the Spirit leads in the direction of helping or serving. Though our outward bodily vessels are aging and declining, our eternal inner man is growing stronger and stronger every day in the Lord. I am not saying that we have to have hands and feet to serve, but for someone like me who travels to foreign lands often, mine are very important to me. It is crucial that I keep them in working order as long as I possibly can.

How are you using your hands and feet? Please don't take them for granted. Our days on this earth are limited, so we had better pursue our callings based upon Matthew 28:18–20. Have you sensed a calling on your life to lead or go on a mission trip? I have come to the conclusion that as long as God calls me, I will continue to go. I truly am not fearful of entering into a hostile county that has been deemed unsafe. There is a switch that flips inside my mind and I press forward, knowing that if I'm called and I'm in God's sweet spot, if He chooses to take me out, then so be it.

What exactly is a mission trip? Ultimately, the purpose of the trip is to demonstrate love; provide food and necessities; build shelter for men and women of all nations; teach God's Word and the sacrifice of His Son to redeem a lost, fallen world; and disciple each as they believe in faith and to then disciple others—all in the name of the One who sent us: Jesus Christ. He made this very clear in the Great

TERRI LYNN SCHMIDT

Commission: "I have been given all authority in heaven and on earth. Therefore, go and make disciples of all the nations, baptizing them in the name of the Father and the Son and the Holy Spirit. Teach these new disciples to obey all the commands I have given you. And be sure of this: I am with you always, even to the end of the age." (Matthew 28:18–20 NLT).

As I laid my head down to get a good night's rest for the next day's journey, I thought of those beautiful hands and feet that are diligently working day and night, helping to recover and clean up after an awful hurricane devastation. Tired as they may be, they persevere, accepting their call to action. How can you use yours for service? Pray for God to show you where to go and who to help. He will call you! There is much need in this world and people who are desperately calling out to you.

> *And how shall they preach unless they are sent? As it is written: "How beautiful are the feet of those who preach the gospel of peace, who bring glad tidings of good things!"*

ROMANS 10:15

HALF-AND-HALF

"Would you like cream with your coffee? Skim, whole, or half-and-half?"

When I drive through for a coffee, I get that question, and my response is the same every time: "I would like half-and-half ... with lots and lots of sugar." Sure, you can taste more of the flavor if you drink your coffee black, but my cup is always fully loaded. Flavored creamers are definitely not a favorite of mine. I want to taste *some* of the coffee, just how I drink it in Honduras—you know, a little coffee with my cream and sugar. First thing in the morning, my feet barely touch the floor before I am taking in a deep breath to smell the fresh brew. If my early alarm goes off, but I haven't heard the perking of the coffee, I lie there in wait.

Any ... minute ... now.

Honestly, I had not planned on writing about coffee creamer. I had another half-and-half in mind. This half-and-half is very familiar to all of us. *So* cliché yet used quite often when trying to help someone determine his or her outlook on life. "Is the glass half full or half empty?" We project our outcome on life based upon the opinion of our carefully chosen response to that silly glass. My opinion? If there is still half a glass of milk remaining, it means I have not finished yet! What's your view on life—half full or half empty? Positive or negative are under scrutiny right now. Choose carefully, or you might just get labeled. Unfortunately.

Funny, isn't it, how one little glass can dictate our choices in life and the way we view them. Each of us is walking a predestined path on this earth. Until we have walked in another person's shoes, we cannot understand their reasoning for the view they choose. Circumstances, hard times, heartbreaks, surroundings, upbringings, and the way we learn to work through them are closely related to our outlook. We do have a choice though. We can choose to not have a label.

Just like adding half-and-half to a black coffee and stirring lightens the brew, the light in Jesus permeates the darkness and brings it into the light. That fact alone should lift our hearts and prod us towards the direction we desperately want to go in. In this case, the glass is ... half full? Who started that cliché to begin with and got us all thinking we had better choose wisely? Oh, good grief! God is the authority of the mind. He is the One who created it.

One morning I pulled myself up off the floor from a self-imposed crying fit, laughing hysterically at myself. I thought, *"Wait a minute! Don't I have a choice here"?* I realized I was actually allowing myself to "wallow" in self-pity. I picked myself up, wiped the tears and mascara from my face, turned on my music, and had a wonderful day. I surprised myself with how quickly I could shift my mind by simply choosing to.

Our minds and choices, left to themselves, will accept the first plight that comes our way if we are unaware of what the Holy Scriptures have to say. Our answers lie within the pages from the front cover to the back. We are challenged to train our minds. We are told to "take captive every thought to make it obedient to Christ" (2 Corinthians 10:5 NIV). Reading and meditating on the Scriptures will train our minds to look at our circumstances in light of all the darkness around us.

No one said that it is easy. That is why we are to *train* our minds, and as we do, we discipline our actions. If we don't like the direction we are headed in, we do have a choice to make. A change that will get our feet moving into the positive. We have a glorious example to follow. Our master, our comforter, our healer, our redeemer, our heavenly Father, our comfort, our protector, our provider. He is the Light, who diminishes the darkness. Instead of giving us half-and-half, He offers to make us whole.

And I saw that wisdom excels folly as light excels darkness.

ECCLESIASTES 2:13 (NASB)

HOMELESS

How did this happen? We never saw this coming.

*Q*uestion after question. Corporations downsize, and people lose their jobs. Many of those individuals are in the latter years of their life with no reserve to see them through. Bills start piling up. The unemployed wait on that next job interview in hopes they will get an offer. No one is hiring. Economic downturn and uncertainties have placed fear in corporate leaders, who have to look out for that bottom line, making it difficult for them to hire one more individual. A vicious cycle continues.

Homeless individuals have lost hope. Security and shelter of a place they once called home is gone. Heaven forbid children are also involved, yet in many cases they certainly are. Though I have not been homeless, our family was asked to evacuate a rental home after the landlord passed and his family wanted to take ownership. Let's not be so quick to judge as to why people find themselves living on the street or under a bridge. There are a multitude of stories and circumstances that have led to their current situation.

I have had a few friends who found themselves homeless on the streets but were able, by the grace of God, to get themselves back on their feet with some sincere help. In turn they began ministries of their own to support homeless shelters and provide food and clothing to those desperately in need.

I was honored to participate with a few of my friends in taking hot plates of food to the men and women living under a bridge near Downtown. A world that I had no idea existed. A village of tents full of people all with a different story as to how and why they came to live in a tent. Beautiful men and women with talents, illnesses, in pain, staying warm with blankets given to them and small fires they manage to burn with very little resources. I desire to take my tent, sleeping bag, and bare necessities to stay with them for a few nights so that I can live their pain and have an understanding of their difficulties. Until we have all walked in each other's shoes in the heartaches of life, we simply cannot have a full understanding.

At Christmastime, I can't help but think of another man who left the comforts of His home, willingly though, and entered into this world knowing that He would become homeless. He entered this world as a baby born in an animal stall because there was not a space available for His birth at an inn. As Jesus began His ministry, He traveled many miles by foot to reach the multitudes to share hope, truth, and eternity. He had many followers who could not get enough of His teachings. When a scribe asked where He was staying, our Lord replied: "Foxes have dens and birds have nests, but the Son of Man has no place to lay His head" (Matthew 8:20).

You see, any of us could become homeless. Most importantly, this earth is not our home. We are passing through to our final destination— heaven. Blessed indeed, are we who have a warm place to rest our bodies, protection from the elements, and a place we call home on this earth. Pray, provide for, and love those who are less fortunate during the seasons of cold winter months as they snuggle down at night under their many blankets waiting for the sun and the Son's return.

> *For this world is not our home; we are looking forward to our everlasting home in heaven.*
>
> HEBREWS 13:14 (TLB)

SWEET SOULS

*S*he travels to the pharmacy in the middle of the night to purchase medicine for her infant. Little baby has a fever. Laundry and ironing are a part of her weekly routine, as it is important that her family's clothing be pressed and polished. Dinner has been poured over and prayed for as it is placed at each table setting. She sacrifices her personal desires and agenda to help with homework and encouragement. Children with broken hearts, broken dreams, and falling tears are safely cuddled in her gentle arms. Wisdom is transferred while sitting at her feet. Smiles adorn her face when she scrolls through the pictures of her memory. Lines on her face deepen yet her heart grows younger. Sweetest souls that we know—Mothers.

As a child and teenager, I remember how involved my mother was in the PTA and how beautiful I thought she was. She won pie contests for having the tallest meringue and got involved with fundraising efforts to help others in the community. Her creative posters and décor adorned our school hallways and my bedroom door. I entered spelling bees and was encouraged by her to try my hand in writing and art competitions. My mother was my number one cheerleader. She encouraged me to pursue my music career and supported me every step of the way. When our family became fragmented and she found herself a single mom, supporting my sisters and me, she sought a job and worked round the clock to purchase our homecoming and prom dresses as well as drill team uniforms. My mother was strong then and she is strong now.

Every one of us has a mother or we simply would not exist. She conceived, carried us in her womb, and birthed us. Maternal, step, adoptive, single, or in-law, all our mothers are endearing. Miles and distance may separate, but the deeply rooted gratitude and love is ever so present. I believe this depth of love between mother and child is one of the strongest bonds known to man. I would lay down my life, stand in front of a runaway train, leap across oncoming traffic, and scream in the face of a grizzly bear to protect my children. Period. One of the toughest things to do is to step aside and let one of my children fall in order to stand, knowing the life lesson will be beneficial to them for their future.

Mother's Day may not be as welcoming to you if you no longer have your mother on this earth or are estranged in your relationship. I sympathize profoundly. Please continue to share your memories and photos. Sweet souls indeed are remembered and honored. Let us reflect upon their love and devotion. We are all better women and men because of their influence. The book of Proverbs describes her well. I pay tribute to my mother here and now: *Happy Mother's Day, Sherry Lynn.*

> *Strength and dignity are her garments; she smiles about the future. She speaks wisely, teaching with gracious love. She looks discretely to the affairs of her household, and she is never lazy. Her children stand up and encourage her, as does her husband, who praises her: "Many women have done wonderful things," he says, "but you surpass all of them!" Charm is deceitful and beauty fades; but a woman who fears the Lord will be praised.*
>
> PROVERBS 31:25–30 (ISV)

WHERE ARE YOU?

*A*s I write you, I am resting against a pillow on the floor of a coffee and vino art bar in Valle de Angeles, Honduras. I am consuming a large terra cotta pot of coffee and taking in the surrounding beauty of purple walls, decorative concrete floors, and amazing pieces of art. I am keenly attuned to all the conversations in the spanish language being spoken all around me. My purpose for this ten-day trip is to minister to the women in local churches, spend time with my children at La Finca Los Niños orphanage, and nurture deeper relationships with the friends here that I have grown to love. I am in love with where I am.

Once while driving down to Austin though, I found myself telling a friend on the phone, "I know where I am going, I just don't know where I am!" I was lost and didn't know which highway direction to take. As I was talking, I had to take an exit and pull over to the side of the road. When I finished my conversation, I was able to get more precise instructions as to where my destination was located. I was on the right path finally. It took me a little longer to get there, but I made it.

Along our walk of faith, many times we hear the most common questions from believers: "How do I know that I am on the *right* path?" We doubt that we have chosen correctly. Yet another question is, "Are we seeking our own will or God's will for our lives"? We may have to pull over, pause, and discover the exact direction to get on the right path. There will be times we will get lost and go astray and not realize it until we hit a roadblock. We have to turn around and seek an alternative route to get back on track.

Our paths consist of good or evil, heaven or hell, right or wrong, mercy or conviction, judgment or compassion, light or darkness, the straight and narrow or wide and destructive. Where are you? When you choose to walk in the Light, Jesus, you will discover that you are walking in God's will and on the right path.

> *Trust in the LORD with all your heart, and lean*
> *not on your own understanding; in all your ways*
> *acknowledge Him, and He shall direct your paths.*

PROVERBS 3:5–6

TERRI LYNN SCHMIDT

RUSTIC

I am such a country girl at heart! Put me in a pair of jeans, cowboy boots, and a cowboy hat, and I feel right at home, *especially* if there is a wide-open field or a horse around. Something about that scene just makes me happy and ready to hop in a car or plane to get there as fast as I can. Can a gal be more in her element? The visual of what I will feast my eyes upon when I arrive? I will encounter a rustic barn, a rustic fence, a rustic saddle, a rustic tractor, and—Lord have mercy—a rustic trailer with rustic siding!

Many times, I have considered residing in the country. It's the one place where I feel totally at ease, where I feel I really belong, where I'm in touch with God's nature. I have ventured this way to write until I find myself here again. The ranch is a familiar friend, as my family and I have been coming here for over twenty years. Out in the fields, past the bottoms, you can find the rustic barn and a tractor left parked to stand the test of time from generations past and for many generations to come. They are weathered and worn with fine lines and cracks displaying their character with secrets and stories to tell of how they survived the storm without losing dignity. Their endurance without wavering has earned them the respect and the much-deserved quality of existing as a rustic icon.

Thanksgiving has come and gone with grace and serenity. We have broken bread together, prayed together, and have thanked our Lord for all the blessings in our lives. The leaves are still changing and falling here at the ranch. Colors are beautifully vibrant, and some trees are bright red, as if on fire. Our next season is quickly approaching, and we have shifted gears and now have focused our attention on the next upcoming season.

As I sit here writing, tomorrow is December 1, and we will begin turning our attention more intently upon someone important who has touched our lives immensely. This person woos our every thought and every action. He understands all too well the meaning of the word *rustic*. He willingly left all of heaven's riches and magnificent shining glory to take on the form of a babe and enter into a broken world, knowing very well that He would be placed in a rustic trough that would serve as a bed for his tiny head.

This tiny head of a little infant, who was to be crowned King above all earthly kings, traded His heavenly crown for another rustic symbol. A crown of thorns. As I walk along the road here on the ranch, I come across many bushes with two-inch thorns and visualize them taking on the shape of a crown that was forced upon the little baby's head when He became an adult. Rustic wood would serve as another symbol for the destiny of this tiny babe. He would not make it into His forties before submitting His complete will to a cruel death on a rustic cross. It would represent death from this world to the transfer of eternal life in another. Here we have unveiled the true beauty in the word *rustic*.

Jesus Christ traded his golden crown for a rustic crown of twisted thorns so that we might one day trade our rustic, worn, weathered crowns for a crown of gold. As you reflect upon the true meaning of the Christmas season, remember that over two thousand years ago, the infant Savior was born into the human realm that we might find life through His adult death. Thank you, baby Jesus.

> *"For unto us a Child is born, unto us a Son is given; and the government shall be upon His shoulder. And His name shall be called Wonderful, Counselor, Mighty God, Everlasting Father, Prince of Peace."*

> ISAIAH 9:6

FINAL DESTINATION

"*W*elcome to Dallas Ft. Worth. Please remain seated with your seatbelt fastened until the plane has come to a complete stop. Please check for personal belongings and when retrieving your luggage from the overheads, please take precaution as your luggage may have shifted during flight. If this is not your final destination, please listen carefully as I call out your connecting gate for your connection. Thank you for flying with American Airlines. We hope you have enjoyed your flight. We look forward to seeing you next time."

Traveling can make you weary! Having layovers and hours of waiting time in between connecting flights can test even the most easy going individual. If you have a direct flight, consider yourself fortunate! You have reached your final destination. Ah, you can breathe. If you have a connecting flight, there is probably still a level of anxiety because you have limited time to gather your belongings, await the river of people to exit the plane, and make a mad dash to your connection gate or terminal change.

"I've Been Everywhere", "I Know Where I'm Going", "I'm Leaving On A Jet Plane", "Flight 309 To Tennessee", and "Fly Over States" are just a few traveling songs from the past. We search for a place far and wide to experience happiness, relaxation, freedom from worry, rejuvenation, and bliss. Some seek these experiences by traveling to an exotic tropical island. For others, they travel by sea, perch on the top of a mountain, or sit next to the ocean. In reality, there is only one final destination that can provide all of these at one time, forever.

With all of our searching we will all come to realize where we are going. Our destination is ultimately found in Heaven. Beautiful mountains, rolling hills, massive oceans, forever blooming flowers as far as our eyes can see. Beauty without end. Everything we seek in this life will be found in this place for eternity. There is only one way to get there though. It requires a saving faith in Jesus Christ. My prayer is that we all run as hard as we can towards the One who has all the answers and is the gateway into this serene place called Heaven. Our eternal life is directly linked to and critically hinges upon Him.

TERRI LYNN SCHMIDT

Jesus said, "I am the way, the truth and the life, no one comes to the Father except through me".

JOHN 14:6

LOST AND FOUND

*L*ittle Jack, a Yorkshire Terrier, succumbed to the pain of his tiny elderly body. His family, recognizing that he had lived a long life full of memories and love, had to make the ever-so-tough decision to relieve Jack of his pain and let him pass into sweet doggie heaven. As many of you know, this is a very heart wrenching and tough decision to make. Jack had made his mark on hearts many years ago, with an interesting story that will be told for family generations to come. For he was lost for forty days and forty nights before he was found!

The story goes: Jack's owners were scheduled to travel on vacation and had left Jack at home to be tended after by close family friends. Unbeknownst to the caretakers, Jack found a way to escape their home and venture out into the day in search of his owners. Being the cute little Yorkshire that he was, he was quickly snatched up by a well-meaning lady who had recently lost her own Yorkie.

The caretakers became frantic upon the discovery of Jack's escape. Signs were posted all through the neighborhood, doors were knocked on, and a huge rescue team was assembled in search of little Jack. The knock then came upon the right door. As the door opened, the lady stood with Jack perched behind her, dressed in female colors! When the rightful owners made eye contact with the woman they knew that she had taken Jack to be her own due to the loss of her own pup who was female. Little Jack began to cry as he recognized his rightful owners, who had returned home, but the dog snatcher insisted that Jack belonged to her.

Long story very short, forty days and forty nights after Jack was lost, snatched, and taken to become a member of another family, a friendly neighborhood policewoman commanded the return of Jack to his rightful owners. Jack was relieved of his pink garments and returned to his nice shades of blue and brown and snuggled down into his own bedding for a restful night's sleep, safe and sound. He had been found. He was right where he belonged.

At the beginning of each new year with hopes for a better tomorrow, we must ask ourselves, are we lost or are we found? Lost by whom and found by whom? By our choice or at the hand of another? If we are familiar with the words to the old hymn "Amazing Grace," then we know the answer to that question. My prayer for all of us is that in the new year we will all be found. Found more faithful, more committed, stronger, more loving—more *everything*. I am grateful to be found and to know where I belong. God is so faithful! There is a significant meaning to forty days and nights not only in Jack's story, but also in Jesus' story.

Then Jesus was led up by the Spirit into the wilderness to be tempted by the devil. And when He had fasted forty days and forty nights, afterward He was hungry. Now when the tempter came to Him, he said, "If You are the Son of God, command that these stones become bread." But He answered and said, "It is written, Man shall not live by bread alone, but by every word that proceeds from the mouth of God."

MATTHEW 4:1–4

ABBA

*D*addy, Big Red, and me … fishing. My turn to get up early and be ready to leave the house for the bridge by 8:00 a.m. sharp! I get dressed and am rearing to go. I awoke early with anticipation of stopping for worms and my very own two-liter bottle of Big Red soda. Over the last several weeks, my two sisters have each had their one-on-one time fishing with Daddy. Going solo with him today, all by myself, is exciting to me! He knows how to make me feel important, like his "one and only little girl."

Those sweet times are memories I will carry with me forever.

Let's give honor to one of the most influential men in our lives, our dads. We would do well to highlight how amazingly impactful our fathers are on our lives. I would have to think this role would be one of the toughest yet rewarding in all of our family units. Daddies and daughters can have a strong bond, but the dad-and-son relationship goes a step further. The son carries the father's last name into the next generation. A father treats his daughter like a princess and pours wisdom and chivalry into his son.

Fathers ensure safety and security. Food on the table and clothing on our backs is not an option; it is a given. Period. If the finances are hard to come by during tough times, dads work double shifts to make sure their family does not skip a beat. Papa bear sits at the head of the dining table. He takes the lead on a hiking adventure and watches the forecast to make certain his family is not placed in harm's way of a dangerous storm. *He* is the umbrella. He carries the torch. He leads his family with intention. Our fathers are strong, committed, and passionate, and will stop at nothing to protect and provide for their family.

Maybe you have or have had an absent father. I understand. For a season in my life I did as well. Earthly fathers can be fallible. As hard as we try not to, we place them on a pedestal. We expect perfection and are disappointed when they cannot be. They were not meant to be. Most of our fathers try their very hardest to be. After they are gone, all we want to remember are the wonderful attributes that made them who they were. Just as my husband was in his daughters' eyes.

There is only One who will never fail us. He is infallible. He is our Abba Father. He has the only perfect relationship with His Son and watches over all His children. He is our ultimate protector and provider. He is a father to the orphan and to the fatherless. He is a husband to the widow. He knows what is best for us and He answers our prayers. He promises to never leave us nor forsake us. He is the "I Am" who will not fail us. It is safe to trust Him and place Him on a pedestal. He is your heavenly Father. Fix your eyes on Him.

> *"This, then, is how you should pray: 'Our Father in heaven: may your name be honored; may your kingdom come; may your will be done on earth as it is in heaven. Give us today the food we need. Forgive us the wrongs we have done, as we forgive the wrongs that others have done to us. Do not bring us to hard testing but keep us safe from the Evil one.'"*

MATTHEW 6:9–13 (GNT)

PRINCE OF PEACE

"Glory to God in the highest, and on earth peace,
good will toward men."

LUKE 2:14 KJV

*O*h, what a beautiful season. At Christmastime we celebrate the birth of our Lord Jesus Christ. Can't you just see it, feel it, and hear it? A crisp starry night, with stillness in the air, ushering in peace on earth. Such a stillness that we can feel it. One star in particular shined high and bright, directing wise men to the exact location of a sweet baby. A bright-eyed child full of wonder. His name was foretold to his earthly father before His birth. Little baby Jesus would grow into adulthood a sinless man who would become God's most precious, spotless sacrificial Lamb. His name was given to Him from the heavens above because He would save the world. Jesus. Peace upon this earth.

Opposing peace in today's time is our bent toward conflict. Turmoil and disaster threaten to choke our ability to find peace. Unstable nations, crime, and deception are at an all-time high. Natural disasters and rumors of war have become daily topics in the news feed. Worrying about situations beyond our control robs us of peace. We are anxious and are too frozen to budge. Every day we struggle to make a concentrated effort to remain calm as we read the headlines. But even through the awfulness, Jesus reigns. He is watching, and He knows our concerns.

If you are a believer in the Holy Trinity, more than likely you have read in the Scriptures about the signs of these modern-day times. We have read about not being caught off guard nor surprised when trouble intensifies. It was foretold to give us a heads-up so we can ready ourselves for whatever comes. As a woman's birthing pain increases with each contraction in anticipation of the child's birth, so our earth also moans and groans under the weight of turmoil as it waits for the return of our Lord.

TERRI LYNN SCHMIDT

For one holy moment in time, the world stood still. There was peace on earth. How many times I have thought about what that night must have been like: Angels announcing His birth with singing and praising. Animals encircling Him, standing and gazing. The magi traveling a long distance, following the star, in all of their glorious attire, in search of the baby. Showering Him with gifts suitable for a king, they kneeled before the child, for they *knew* He was worthy to be King! Mary, exhausted from childbirth, and Joseph, in awe of the attention his child was receiving, watching in silence. Oh, what a holy night! It was the night of our Savior's birth.

If peace has escaped you and you have become gripped with fear and worry, rest assured: Even through all of the trials and tribulations this world brings your way, your peace can still and always will be found in Jesus. Thank you, Father, for the gift of Your Son, King Jesus.

> *"These things I have spoken to you, that in Me you may have peace. In the world you will have tribulation; but be of good cheer, I have overcome the world."*

> JOHN 16:33

MERCY

*M*ercy, Father, mercy. Please have mercy. We understand that we are all deserving of punishment for our actions in direct response to our obedience and Your ordained authority. But for those who are not deserving and are being persecuted and ridiculed for something beyond their control and or unknowingly performed by them, please have mercy. Father, your ways are not our ways nor are Your thoughts our thoughts. In Your compassionate authority, mercy for the innocent is our plea.

Returning from the Amazon River yesterday afternoon has sent me into a tail spin of thought and emotion as I was certain it would. Though I had been on a mission trip before down the Amazon back in 2006, this experience was quite different. Our team, lead by the director of Amazon Outreach, ventured into a different area of the river to a city named Anori. Our team of all women were asked to host a 3-day women's conference at a Presbyterian church. Brazilian women traveled from hours away to attend and local women of the church hosted them in their homes. There were 150 women of all ages in attendance. Our conference was based on Ephesians 6:14-17 teaching on the Full Armor of God.

Although I have developed a passion through my mission travels, into a variety of countries, for women to understand that we were all created in the image of God and carry the same concerns globally, it was the children that drew me in and captured my attention on this particular trip. The impressionable innocent children. Ironic considering, I had prepared my lesson on addressing the Breastplate of Righteousness for the women as our humble dedicated sister team members poured their hearts ministering to the children by teaching bible lessons. As we prayed over the children one morning before they headed out of the sanctuary, it occurred to me. These little ones were the generation for change to take place for the future. Their minds, their bible studies, their character, wisdom, integrity, and commitment to righteous living would be the pivotal turning point in reaching their community and their country for change.

Innocent children. Father, have mercy. Mercy for one young man in particular. Gerdeson and his little brother. Gerdeson lives in a smaller village called Nazarene, 5 hours down the Amazon from Anori. This village was spiritually oppressed and we were the first group to visit them besides the Pastor who had begun visiting them 2 years ago. While walking through the village, 4 of us ladies were directed to one house in particular. A home built high off the ground on stilts for when the river rises just as the other homes up and down the footpath. We were specifically asked to visit this home by a fellow team member who was a doctor on the trip with us. As we approached the house Gerdeson's mother began to call obscenities and would not allow our visit. When she saw our American wrapped candy come through her window by her son, she appeared at the window and asked us inside.

An hour later through many tears, we learned the story of Angelica's life with her husband and the man she was living with at the moment. While 2 of our women were ministering to her with scripture through an interpreter, I visited with Gerdeson and taught him some English words and phrases. He was impressed by my aiming ability to shoot a dart through his toy gun at the make-do target he had set up on the tiny dining table. To see his precious eyes and gentle smile after receiving confirmations of his pronunciations, it would so hard to accept that the man in their home beat him and his little brother because he was angry and did not like them. His little brother is 1 year old. How could this sweet young man still display a smile and eagerness to learn with all he is living day in and day out? Mercy, Father, mercy. We spent as much time with them as we could for as long as it took to help Angelica and her sons process the understanding of God's forgiveness and love. As we prayed, Gerdeson wrapped his sweet arm around my neck and laid his head on my back as I rocked him to and fro. God laid hold of his young heart.

How do we get back in a boat and leave this precious family and the rest? Trust me. It isn't easy at all. The river infested chiggers and mosquitoes made it a little easier, as well as the alligator and anaconda stories. Piranhas in the waters around our boat also gave us a little push out back onto the river. After showers and moments of sharing our thoughts, deep emotions of all the needs still not met there can only be drawn to one conclusion. God is still on the throne and still in control. His commission to us through the words spoken through Him to His disciples are equally as important. Go into all the nations and share the news of the gospel of Christ. Only and THEN only after all have heard, will Jesus make His return for God's people. God in all His mercy will not allow one person be left untold or uninformed in regards to their salvation and forgiveness from sin.

Here we are back on spoiled American soil with our hot showers and comfy bedding. Where we hear the gospel over and over with a church on every corner and we still pick and choose what or when we want to act upon our faith. There are nations that have not heard one word. For those nations I pray, "Father, please have mercy." Mercy as they wait for those obedient to the command to go into all the nations carrying the good news. Mercy on the children who are living in conditions not of their own choosing. Circumstances beyond their control. Waiting for hope for their future. Lord. Please. Have. Mercy.

> *Return, O Lord, deliver me! Oh, save me for Your mercies sake!*

> PSALM 6:4

TERRI LYNN SCHMIDT

LOVE

ove is such a beautiful feeling. Love is definitely in the air, as I have seen so many engagements take place this past year. One in particular is my daughter Hillary to her fiancé, Tanner. What a sweet time of watching two young people work together to plan their future as Mr. and Mrs. Nelson. Harry, my late husband, would have been so proud. Joining two families as one is an ultimate joy within a family's life.

One morning, I decided I was going to go back and revisit letters and cards I had exchanged with my husband and letters Harry had written to his mother and father from college. There were also cards from my daughters written to their dad, all of them describing love in different forms. The love between a mother and her son, the love between a daughter and her father, the love between a father and his son, and the love between wife and husband. Everyone has one foundation in place that is universal—expressions of love. What joy filled my heart to go back and reread the expressions of love written in the letters and cards.

Four Greek words describe different types of love. I know you probably have heard or read about each one, but let's revisit them:

Agape love: Love in the verb category. An unconditional love that sees beyond another's flaws and loves anyway. A sacrificial love that gives expecting nothing in return. It is a committed and chosen love demonstrated by our behavior toward each other. This is the love most sought after in relation to marriage.

Phileo love: Love in the noun category. A love that is most common among friends. This love is based on our feelings toward each other. We may not have an agape love toward our friends, but we demonstrate our love for them by choosing and committing to spend our time with them.

Storge love: This love is an example of a parent's love

for a child. Storge love can be felt toward our friends, and we build a solid friendship based upon it. Also, what is desired in an agape love relationship can be built into the storge relationship, which sets the stage for a beautiful marriage built upon a committed, unconditional love with your "best friend."

Eros love: A romantic and passionate love based upon feelings. Usually a selfish love based around what the other person can do to fulfill our selfish needs or desires. This type of love can fall away when the "feeling" of love disappears without a foundation built upon an agape love in harmony with a storge love.

We all fall into one or two of these categories at some point. In our lifetime we will experience them all. I bet you can categorize the relationships in your life right now based upon each type of love.

I personally have experienced all four, sometimes all occurring simultaneously with my husband, children, family, and friends. When we say I love you, we are speaking the truth based upon one of these types of love. Even when we don't particularly like someone, there is a presence of love toward that person. There is a very powerful reason why and a strong force behind that reason: God. God created love. He is love, and He created every one of our brains, where our emotions reside. So why do we use the symbol of the heart to express love? I felt led to do some research and share my findings with you.

The heart was adopted as the symbol of love in the fifteenth century. In the sixteenth century, it became most popular in Europe. As one legend goes, the story of St. Valentine was based on a true story of love between a woman and a man, St. Valentine, in Venice, Italy. She stood on the top of the bridge and would call to her love, who was imprisoned in a building just across the waterway. I have stood on that bridge. The prison is still there. (A little trivia: The color for the heart symbol, red, was selected by renowned artists because of their love for the red color of the cardinal bird.)

In ancient days, with the heart being located in the center of the body, some people believed it to be the center of emotions. Obviously, these people did not have a clear understanding of our brain, how it works, and that love is fashioned in the brain, although the brain and heart affect each other. With love being a very strong emotion, the people chose the heart symbol to represent love. Even though our thoughts and feelings of love in our brains do set our hearts a-thumping! Before I write a complete novel on love, I will leave you with a Scripture about this powerful word:

"Many waters

cannot quench

the flame of love."

SONG OF SOLOMON 8:7 (TLB)

Taken when the girls and I went to Mexico in 2012.
We had a private memorial to Harry on the beach

God gave this sign in the clouds
as a gift one day on my walk in Austin, Texas